little dish™

Favourites Cookbook

For Monty & Ridley

little dish™

Favourites Cookbook

Hillary Graves

HODDER &
STOUGHTON

First published in Great Britain in 2010 by Hodder & Stoughton
An Hachette UK company

1

Copyright © Little Dish 2010

The right of Little Dish to be identified as the Author of the Work has been
asserted by it in accordance with the Copyright, Designs and Patents Act
1988.

A CIP catalogue record for this title is available from the British Library

ISBN 978 1 444 70417 4

Illustrations by Claudio Vecchio at Pearlfisher

Design by Lisa Pettibone

Typeset in ITC Souvenir and Fresco

Printed and bound in Italy by L.E.G.O. Spa

Hodder & Stoughton policy is to use papers that are natural, renewable and
recyclable products and made from wood grown in sustainable forests.
The logging and manufacturing processes are expected to conform to the
environmental regulations of the country of origin.

Hodder & Stoughton Ltd
338 Euston Road
London NW1 3BH
www.hodder.co.uk

Contents

Introduction to Little Dish

In 2006 I co-founded Little Dish with my business partner, John Stapleton. We set out to make a range of fresh, healthy food for toddlers and young children made from 100 per cent natural ingredients and no added salt or sugar.

We knew that establishing healthy eating habits at an early age is crucial, but we also recognised that home cooking every night of the week can be challenging for busy families. We wanted to replicate what parents would make in their kitchens if they had enough time. Now our Little Dish fresh meals are trading in Tesco, Sainsbury's, Waitrose and Ocado.com and we have recently added fresh baby food to the range.

One of the most important parts of recipe development at Little Dish is 'kid-testing'. We know it doesn't matter how healthy a meal is if your child won't eat it. So we spend a lot of time testing our meals on toddlers and fussy eaters. My children, Monty (as I write this, he's three) and Ridley (11 months), lead the tasting panel.

Since we launched four years ago, parents have called and written every week asking us for our recipes. Many requested we write a cookbook, and so we are excited to be finally publishing the *Little Dish Favourites Cookbook*.

The recipes in this book are specially designed for time-challenged parents who want to feed their children nutritious, home-cooked food but don't have hours to spend in the kitchen. While there are days you'll want to use our freshly prepared meals from the chilled aisle of the supermarket, there are times when we all like to make homemade. And to have our children join in the making. Every recipe in this book has been taste tested by kids and proved very popular with our tasting panels.

Many of these recipes are easily made ahead of time for convenience and can be made in big batches so leftover portions can be frozen for quick access on really busy nights. Each recipe has a chart detailing the number of servings, preparation time and cooking time, and also an indication of how simple it is to make. The fewer the number of tomatoes, the easier it is:

🍅 Simple

🍅 🍅 Straightforward

🍅 🍅 🍅 Small degree of complexity

We've divided the book into three main sections. **First Tastes** includes ten very easy purées for weaning, when you are first introducing your children to solids, as well as some more complex recipes for the second stage of weaning. The majority of the book is filled with a lovely selection of **Family Dishes**, which are all very popular in my household and were loved by both children and adults in our recipe-testing sessions. We finish off with **Treats & Puddings**, which include delicious but not overly sweet desserts.

We hope many of these recipes will become staples in your household: so easy that you quickly know them by heart, and so delicious that your children ask for them by name.

HILLARY GRAVES
Co-founder of Little Dish

First Tastes

There once was a wobbly cow
Who kept falling over somehow
But a meal that was balanced
So improved her talents
She can ride a unicycle now

At Little Dish we believe food shouldn't be older than your baby. Baby-food jars, pots and pouches (sold in the nappy aisle of the supermarket as opposed to the chilled aisle) can have up to 18 months' shelf-life. The occasional jar or pot can be convenient when you are on the go, but most feeding occasions for babies take place in the home, and in these cases try to serve fresh food when possible.

Proof that purées are easy

I had never made a purée until I had my first baby. And I found the thought of it a bit overwhelming – not necessarily the purée itself but the fact that I was making something for my tiny baby. Would I do it right? Would it be cooked enough? Would it be the right texture? Would he choke?

I think for a lot of mothers there can be this confidence issue: perhaps you are doing it for the first time or you're not exactly sure how to get started. The other barrier is, of course, time. We all know that once you have a baby (never mind more than one), there is no more time.

With all that in mind, the first part of this book gives you ten very simple purées, which are perfect first foods for your baby, as well as a 1-2-3 guide to making them. (With leftovers to store in the freezer.)

When to start?

The first question is when to start your baby on solids. I found this confusing and I got mixed advice – most people said six months, but some suggested as early as four months.

The World Health Organisation guidelines recommend that weaning should be started at six months to allow a baby's digestive system sufficient time to mature. According to WHO, if you can wait until six months, you are allowing your baby's kidneys and gut to develop as much as possible before introducing foods that might make them susceptible to allergies later on.

Ask your health visitor for his or her perspective on this, especially if your baby is not yet six months old but still seems hungry after a milk feed or is suddenly waking in the night. In my case, I weaned my first baby at five months because he was hungry. Milk was no longer doing the trick, so we started topping up with a bit of rice cereal. With my second baby things ran more smoothly and he was able to wait until six months on the dot. Every baby is different. Trust your instincts and use your health visitor as a resource.

Here are some signs your baby may be ready for solids:

- Your baby is holding his or her head up – before eating food from a spoon, your baby should be able to sit upright and hold his or her head in a steady position.
- Your baby shows an interest in food, watching you at mealtimes and sometimes reaching out for your food.
- Your baby is hungry after feeding.
- Your baby wakes more often during the night for feeds or the time between feeds gets shorter.

Weaning: A few simple guidelines

After six months, milk can no longer satisfy all a baby's nutritional needs. The baby's stores of nutrients, such as iron, start to run out, which is why you need to start introducing new foods. Moving on to solid foods also helps your baby develop the muscles necessary for chewing and, eventually, speech.

There are a few simple guidelines to weaning which you should be familiar with before feeding your baby for the first time:

1 Before preparing and cooking food, make sure your hands are clean, as well as all the cooking utensils, preparation surfaces, pots and pans.
2 The first foods introduced should have a thin, smooth consistency (just slightly thicker than milk).
3 Never add salt or sugar to foods for babies; even if the food tastes bland to you, it will be fine for your baby.
4 Start by offering small amounts, about 1–2 teaspoons of purée.
5 Introduce only one new food at a time and continue for two or three days so you can monitor any reaction.
6 Do not try to introduce new foods if your baby is tired, over-hungry or teething.
7 Never leave your baby alone while he or she is eating because of the risk of choking.
8 Offer cooled boiled water to drink in between feeds if necessary, and encourage drinks to be taken from a beaker cup during meals.

For both my children, I introduced solids at their 11 a.m. feed, after they had had some milk (so they weren't starving) but midway through their feed so they were still hungry.

I started with a few spoonfuls of butternut squash purée; carrot or sweet potatoes are also great options. I chose to go with vegetables first, but gradually I introduced apples, bananas, pears and mangoes.

One thing to remember is that the purée period does not last very long, it is just a way to get your baby to move on from milk. Many parents (including me with my first baby) make the mistake of puréeing foods for months and months, when actually you want to start introducing texture and lumps as early as seven months: that's Stage 2, in the next part of this chapter (page 26).

Stage One

This selection of purées gives you sufficient variety for the first stage of weaning. What's more, the list is short enough that you can master these recipes and become an expert in making homemade baby food very quickly.

These recipes use carrot, sweet potato, butternut squash, apple, pear, mango, banana, avocado, green beans, courgette, peas and porridge – all great first foods for a baby.

Getting the right kit

The trick to keeping purées simple is one essential piece of kit: a hand blender. This is very easy to use (and store) and will quickly become indispensable in making food for your baby. Also useful are ice-cube trays for freezing leftovers in small sizes you can quickly thaw.

I recommend steaming vegetables and fruit in order to retain the most nutrients possible. The easiest method is to use a perforated steaming basket that folds flat when not in use. Just put vegetables or fruit in the steam basket and place on top of a pan of simmering water.

You'll want to use a soft plastic spoon (as opposed to a hard metal one) to feed your baby, and I find the flexible plastic bibs with a catch-all at the bottom to be by far the best, which you'll especially appreciate once your baby starts finger food.

Carrot Purée

INGREDIENTS

6 large carrots

- Wash and peel the carrots and cut into 3 cm (just over 1in) pieces.

- Place the carrots in a steaming basket in a pan of lightly boiling water, ensuring the water level is below the vegetables. Cover with a well-fitting lid (to help retain nutrients) and steam for 12–15 minutes, until tender. Set the carrots aside in a bowl to cool slightly and reserve the cooking liquid.

- Purée the carrots and 3–4 tablespoons of the reserved liquid (or breast milk or formula, if preferred) with a hand blender. Use more liquid if needed for a smoother consistency.

SIMPLICITY:

MAKES:
4 portions

PREP TIME:
5 minutes

COOKING TIME:
12–15 minutes

⭐ **Keep in the refrigerator for up to 2 days, or freeze in ice-cube trays for up to 30 days.**

Sweet Potato Purée

SIMPLICITY:

MAKES:
4 portions

PREP TIME:
5 minutes

COOKING TIME:
45 minutes

INGREDIENTS

2 sweet potatoes

• Preheat the oven to 220°C/425°F/Gas 7. Wash and scrub the sweet potatoes. Prick with a fork and place on a baking tray.

• Bake for 45 minutes, until tender and the skin is wrinkled. The potatoes should be easy to pierce with the tip of a knife. Set them aside to cool before handling.

• Using your fingers, peel off the skin. Cut the flesh into small pieces, put in a bowl and add 1–2 tablespoons of water, breast milk or formula, as preferred. Mash well with a fork or purée with a hand blender.

Keep in the refrigerator for up to 2 days, or freeze in ice-cube trays for up to 30 days.

Butternut Squash Purée

INGREDIENTS

1 butternut squash (roughly 500g/1lb)

- Preheat the oven to 190°C/375°F/Gas 5. Cut the squash in half and remove the seeds. Place the halves cut-side down in a baking tray and pour 100ml (6 tablespoons) water into the bottom of the tray.

- Bake the squash for about 45 minutes, until tender to the touch of a fork. Remove from the oven and set aside to cool slightly.

- Spoon out the flesh and place it in a bowl. Add 1–2 tablespoons of water, breast milk or formula, as preferred. Mash well with a fork or purée with a hand blender.

SIMPLICITY:

MAKES:
5 portions

PREP TIME:
5 minutes

COOKING TIME:
45 minutes

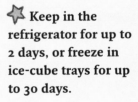 **You can now find peeled and diced butternut squash in many supermarkets. Simply steam for 12–15 minutes and purée.**

Keep in the refrigerator for up to 2 days, or freeze in ice-cube trays for up to 30 days.

Apple Purée

⭐ **Keep in the refrigerator for up to 2 days, or freeze in ice-cube trays for up to 30 days.**

INGREDIENTS

6 medium apples (Braeburn or similar)

• Wash, core and peel the apples and cut into quarters.

• Place the apples in a steaming basket in a pan of lightly boiling water, ensuring the water level is below the fruit. Cover with a well-fitting lid (to help retain nutrients) and steam for 12 minutes, until tender. Set the apples aside to cool slightly and reserve the liquid.

• Purée the apples and 1–2 tablespoons of the reserved liquid (or breast milk or formula, if preferred) with a hand blender. Use more liquid if necessary for a smoother consistency.

Pear Purée

INGREDIENTS

4 ripe pears

- Wash, core and peel the pears and cut into quarters.

- Place the pears in a steaming basket in a pan of lightly boiling water, ensuring the water level is below the fruit. Cover with a well-fitting lid (to help retain nutrients) and steam for 12 minutes, until tender. Set the pears aside to cool slightly and reserve the liquid.

- Purée the pears and 1–2 tablespoons of the reserved liquid (or breast milk or formula, if preferred) with a hand blender. Use more liquid if necessary for a smoother consistency.

SIMPLICITY:

MAKES:
4 portions

PREP TIME:
2 minutes

COOKING TIME:
12 minutes

Keep in the refrigerator for up to 2 days, or freeze in ice-cube trays for up to 30 days.

Mango Purée

MAKES:
3 portions

PREP TIME:
5 minutes

COOKING TIME:
4–6 minutes

⭐ **Keep in the refrigerator for up to 2 days, or freeze in ice-cube trays for up to 30 days.**

INGREDIENTS

1 medium mango

• Slice the flesh of the mango away from the stone. Scoop out the flesh with a spoon or knife and cut into medium-sized chunks.

• Place the mango in a steaming basket in a pan of lightly boiling water, ensuring the water level is below the fruit. Cover with a well-fitting lid (to help retain nutrients) and steam for 4–6 minutes, until tender.

• Purée the mango with a hand blender (additional liquid is not usually needed).

Avocado & Banana Purée

INGREDIENTS

1 large ripe avocado
1 large ripe banana

- Cut the avocado lengthways, remove the stone and spoon the flesh into a bowl. Mash well with a fork.

- Peel the banana, cut into small pieces on a chopping board and mash with a fork. Add to the bowl with the avocado.

- Add 1–2 tablespoons of water, breast milk or formula to thin the purée as necessary.

SIMPLICITY:

MAKES:
2 portions

PREP TIME:
5 minutes

COOKING TIME:
no cooking reqired

Hard avocados ripen more quickly if placed in a brown paper bag with a banana for a day or two.

Keep in the refrigerator for up to 1 day.

Green Bean Purée

SIMPLICITY:

MAKES:
2-3 portions

PREP TIME:
5 minutes

COOKING TIME:
12 minutes

⭐ **Keep in the refrigerator for up to 2 days, or freeze in ice-cube trays for up to 30 days.**

INGREDIENTS

225g (8 oz) green beans

• Wash and trim off the tips of the beans.

• Place the beans in a steaming basket in a pan of lightly boiling water, ensuring the water level is below the vegetables. Cover with a well-fitting lid (to help retain nutrients) and steam for 12 minutes, until tender. Reserve the liquid. Cool the beans by running cold water over them.

• Using a hand blender, purée the beans with 120ml (8 tablespoons) of the reserved liquid. Use some of the cooking liquid (or breast milk or formula, if preferred) for a smoother consistency.

Courgette & Pea Purée

INGREDIENTS

1 large courgette
280g (10 oz) frozen peas

- Wash the courgette and cut into thick rounds (do not peel).

- Place the courgette in a steaming basket in a pan of lightly boiling water, ensuring the water level is below the vegetables. Cover with a well-fitting lid (to help retain nutrients) and steam for 2–3 minutes, then add the peas and continue steaming for 8–10 minutes.

- Put the courgette and peas in a bowl and allow to cool slightly, then purée with a hand blender. (As courgettes have a higher water content than many vegetables, you should not need to add extra liquid.)

SIMPLICITY:

MAKES:
4 portions

PREP TIME:
2 minutes

COOKING TIME:
10–15 minutes

☆ **Keep in the refrigerator for up to 2 days, or freeze in ice-cube trays for up to 30 days.**

Super Porridge

SIMPLICITY:

MAKES:
4 portions

PREP TIME:
2 minutes

COOKING TIME:
10 minutes

Oats are one of the most nutritious grains you can give to your baby, as well as safe because of the low risk of allergy. Additionally, because of their high fibre content, oats do not cause constipation, which can happen with rice cereal. A warm bowl of porridge is the perfect breakfast for the whole family, including your baby. You can serve it plain or add flaxseed and fruit for extra vitamins and nutrients. My 11-month-old loves this recipe with bananas and blueberries. Purée very smooth for younger babies, but between 7 and 8 months they should be fine with a bit of texture.

⭐ **Leftovers keep in the refrigerator for up to 24 hours. Reheat in a saucepan over low heat or in a microwave.**

INGREDIENTS

90g (3 oz) porridge oats
470 ml (16 fl. oz) whole milk
1-2 teaspoons flaxseed
$\frac{1}{2}$ banana, sliced
50g (2 oz) blueberries

• Put the oats and milk in a saucepan and bring to the boil.

• Turn the heat down and simmer for 10 minutes, until the porridge is creamy.

• Remove from the heat and add the flaxseed, banana and blueberries. Use a hand blender to mix together.

When your baby is comfortable with lumps, simply chop blueberries and bananas (or any fruit) and add to porridge.

Stage Two

The first part of this chapter illustrates how simple making purées can be, and I hope your baby is now enjoying his or her first tastes.

- Once your baby has been eating fruit and vegetable purées for a few weeks and is at least seven months old, start to introduce a slight texture to the food and eventually get your baby used to lumps.
- Between seven and eight months, you can introduce protein, including chicken, fish, lentils and meat.

At this stage in your baby's diet, fresh food is even more important. Meat and fish out of a jar taste awful because of high-heating treatments used to achieve a long shelf-life. If you truly want your baby to have a love and appreciation of good food, it is best to introduce him or her to real tastes as soon as you can. These next recipes are easy, baby- and toddler-friendly, and perfect for the second stage of weaning. Just make sure not to introduce more than one new ingredient to your baby at a time so you can monitor any kind of reaction, allergic or otherwise.

The first time you give these Stage 2 recipes to your baby, you can purée them down to a smooth consistency. However, as soon as you are ready to introduce texture, a quick buzz with the hand blender will be all that's needed, or simply mash the food with a fork. Just make sure, as you feed your baby, that there are no big pieces of meat or vegetables he or she could choke on. Pay attention to each spoonful to catch any pieces of food that haven't been adequately mashed.

Foods to avoid in the first year

Avoid giving your baby the following foods before he or she is 12 months old: honey, eggs, nuts, shellfish, sugar and salt. Also, your baby should not drink cow's milk before 12 months, though it can be used as an ingredient in cooking. Talk to your health visitor about any ingredients you are not sure about, especially if allergies run in your family.

If at first your baby doesn't like it, try again

When a new food is rejected, don't be discouraged or frustrated. Sometimes it can take three, four or even five tries before your baby likes it. The important thing is not to give up after the first refusal.

Also, it is easy to get caught in the trap of giving your baby sweet options such as fruit or yoghurt if the savoury gets rejected. Try not to. Your baby is smart and will soon realise that by rejecting the first course they will get what they are really after. Persevere through the complaining. As a last resort, mix the savoury with the sweet in an effort to get their main course down.

Developing your baby's palate

As with all baby food, never add salt or sugar. Use various spices to develop flavours. Fresh garlic, oregano, rosemary, thyme, basil, dill and mint are all great options. It's also helpful to make your own salt-free vegetable or chicken stock (pages 29 and 30), because many of the shop-bought versions have high sodium (salt) levels. Make a big batch and freeze individual portions for convenience. If you use shop-bought, look for salt-free varieties.

Introduce new tastes gradually. For example, mix a small amount of chicken stock, about a tablespoon, into your baby's vegetable purées for a week or so before giving them Chicken Casserole (page 34). I did this with both my children and it worked well.

How much food to give your baby

Your baby will guide you. Babies let you know if they want more, usually by complaining or crying when the bowl is empty, or, if they have had their fill, by turning their head or pushing the spoon away. For the most part you can feel confident your baby knows how much he or she needs.

These recipes yield more than you are likely to need at once so that you can refrigerate or freeze the excess. Freeze well-puréed food in ice-cube trays and reheat a few blocks at a time. As you move on to more complex recipes with greater texture, it may be easier to freeze individual portion sizes in small containers.

Homemade Vegetable Stock

This stock is easy and quick to make. You can vary the vegetables according to what you have on hand.

INGREDIENTS

1 onion, peeled and quartered
2 carrots, roughly chopped
1 parsnip, roughly chopped
2 sticks celery, roughly chopped
1 leek, green and white parts roughly chopped
1 garlic clove
1 bay leaf
1.5 litres (2¹/₂ pints) water

- Put all the ingredients in a large saucepan, cover with a lid and bring to the boil. Then the heat down and simmer, uncovered, for 30 minutes.

- Strain into a bowl, discarding the vegetables. Set aside to cool, then refrigerate or freeze.

SIMPLICITY:

MAKES:
1 litre (1 ³/₄ pints)

PREP TIME:
10 minutes

COOKING TIME:
30 minutes

This stock keeps in the refrigerator for 1–2 days or in the freezer for up to 60 days.

It's very handy to freeze stocks in ice-cube trays so you can thaw small amounts at a time.

Homemade Chicken Stock

SIMPLICITY:

MAKES:
about 2 litres (3 ½ pints)

PREP TIME:
10 minutes

COOKING TIME:
1 ½ - 4 hours

This recipe calls for a whole chicken, but you can easily use the leftover carcass from a roast chicken as an alternative. I use a whole chicken for two reasons. First, it makes a lovely tasting stock, and second, I find it a convenient way to cook chicken breasts, which can then be used in Chicken Casserole (page 34) or Chicken Pasta Bake (page 64). The dark meat works well in Creamy Chicken Curry (page 74).

⭐ **This stock keeps in the refrigerator for a week or in the freezer for up to 60 days.**

INGREDIENTS

1 whole chicken, skin on
1 carrot, roughly chopped
1 onion, peeled and halved
1 leek, roughly chopped
1 bay leaf

- Remove the giblets from the chicken, if there are any. Give the chicken a quick rinse under cold water, then put it in a large pot and cover with cold water. Put a lid on the pan, bring to the boil, then turn the heat down and simmer. Skim off the foam and add the vegetables and bay leaf.

- Continue to simmer, uncovered, for an hour, then carefully remove the chicken from the pot, carve off the breasts and return the carcass to the pot. Simmer for a minimum of 30 minutes more, or up to an additional 2 $1/2$ hours if possible. Strain the stock and set aside to cool, then skim off any fat. Store in the refrigerator or freezer.

It's very handy to freeze stocks in ice-cube trays so you can thaw small amounts at a time.

Lentil Casserole

SIMPLICITY:

MAKES:
8 children's portions

PREP TIME:
20 minutes

COOKING TIME:
30 minutes

Lentils are a great way to introduce protein, and the flavour in this dish is appealing to both babies and toddlers.

INGREDIENTS

2 potatoes, peeled and diced

1 sweet potato, peeled and diced

Knob of unsalted butter

Dash of milk

¹/₂ onion, diced

¹/₂ leek, sliced

1 teaspoon dried mixed herbs

1 tablespoon olive oil

500ml (18 fl. oz) water

175g (6 oz) red lentils

1 tablespoon tomato purée

90g (3 oz) Cheddar cheese, grated

⭐ **Keeps in the refrigerator for 2 days or in the freezer for 30 days.**

- Preheat the oven to 180°C/350°F/Gas 4.

- Put the potato and sweet potato in a pan, cover with water
  and boil gently until tender. Drain and mash with the butter
  and a dash of milk.

- While the potatoes are boiling, cook the onion, leek and
  herbs in the olive oil in a saucepan until the onion is soft.
  Add the water, lentils and tomato purée, and cook for about
  12 minutes, until the lentils are soft.

- Place in a casserole dish, layer the mash on top and finally
  sprinkle with the cheese. Bake in the oven for 30 minutes,
  until the cheese is bubbling and golden.

- The consistency should be fine for toddlers, but purée or
  mash to the appropriate consistency for your baby.

Chicken Casserole

SIMPLICITY:

MAKES:
8 children's portions

PREP TIME:
25 minutes

COOKING TIME:
1 hour 15 minutes

This chicken casserole is hearty and healthy. Both my children loved it when they were babies, and it is also a favourite with toddlers and older children. The sweet potato and leek create a lovely combination of flavours so you don't miss the salt.

INGREDIENTS
½ onion, peeled and diced
1 garlic clove, finely chopped
½ leek, chopped
Pinch of dried mixed herbs
2 tablespoon olive oil
2 x 150g (5 oz) cooked boneless skinless chicken
    breasts, diced
1 sweet potato, peeled and diced
2 potatoes, peeled and diced
1 carrot, peeled and diced
560ml (1 pint) chicken stock (page 30) or shop-bought
    with no added salt

- Preheat the oven to 180°C/350°F/Gas 4.

- In an ovenproof casserole, cook the onions, garlic, leek and herbs in the olive oil over a medium heat until softened. Add the chicken, remaining vegetables and the stock, then bring to the boil then turn the heat down and simmer for 15 minutes.

- Cover and transfer to the preheated oven and bake for 1 hour.

- Purée or mash to the appropriate consistency for your baby or cut into small pieces for your toddler.

Keeps in the refrigerator for 2 days or in the freezer for 30 days.

Use the chicken breast from the stock-making on page 30.

Fish Bake

SIMPLICITY:

MAKES:
6 children's portions

PREP TIME:
20 minutes

COOKING TIME:
45 minutes

Fish can be a strong taste for babies. To introduce them to the flavour, I suggest you use a mild fish such as cod or haddock.

INGREDIENTS

2 x 150g (5 oz) cod or haddock fillets

1 potato, peeled and diced

1 sweet potato, peeled and diced

1 carrot, peeled and diced

Knob of butter

Dash of milk

½ onion, peeled and diced

1 tablespoon olive oil

100g (4 oz) Cheddar cheese, grated

225ml (8 fl. oz) vegetable stock (page 29) or shop-bought with no added salt

- Preheat the oven to 180°C/350°F/Gas 4.

- Check that the cod fillets are completely free of bones, using your fingers to feel for them, then rinse and pat dry. Oil a large piece of foil, place the fillets on it, skin-side down, then wrap the foil loosely around the fish to enclose it. Transfer to a tray and bake in the oven for 12–15 minutes, until fish is completely cooked.

- While the fish is baking, put the potato, sweet potato and carrot in a pan, cover with water and boil gently, until tender. Drain and mash together with the butter and milk.

- Meanwhile, cook the onion in the olive oil for a few minutes until soft. When the fish is cooked, remove from the oven and flake with a fork, discarding the skin. Mix the fish in with the onions.

- In an ovenproof dish, layer the ingredients, starting with half the fish, then half the mash. Make a second layer of fish, a second layer of potato and finish off with the cheese. Pour the vegetable stock over the dish and bake in the oven for 45 minutes, until the cheese is bubbling and golden.

- Purée or mash to the appropriate consistency for your baby or cut into small pieces for your toddler.

Keeps in the refrigerator for 2 days or in the freezer for 30 days.

Broccoli & Cauliflower Cheese

SIMPLICITY:

MAKES:
4 children's portions

PREP TIME:
5 minutes

COOKING TIME:
10–15 minutes

This is my favourite way to introduce babies and toddlers to broccoli and cauliflower, which are full of vitamins and antioxidants.

INGREDIENTS

75g (3 oz) broccoli, cut into small florets

100g (4 oz) cauliflower, cut into small florets

20g (³/₄ oz) unsalted butter

20g (³/₄ oz) plain flour

200ml (7 fl. oz) whole milk

25g (1 oz) freshly grated Parmesan cheese

25g (1 oz) Cheddar cheese, grated

- Steam the broccoli and cauliflower florets for about 8–10 minutes, until tender.

- Meanwhile, make the cheese sauce. Melt the butter in a saucepan and then gradually stir in the flour. Slowly whisk in the milk so that you have a smooth white sauce, bring to the boil, then turn the heat down and simmer for 2–3 minutes. When the sauce thickens, remove the saucepan from the heat and stir in the cheese.

- Pour the cheese sauce over the broccoli and cauliflower florets.

- Purée or mash to the appropriate consistency for your baby or cut into small pieces for your toddler.

☆ Keeps in the refrigerator for 2 days or in the freezer for 30 days.

Easy Bolognese

SIMPLICITY:

MAKES:
8 children's portions

PREP TIME:
15 minutes

COOKING TIME:
1 hour

A perfect first Bolognese for babies and toddlers and a healthy way to introduce beef, which is full of zinc and iron. It's also tasty enough for the whole family if you don't have time to make Proper Bolognese (page 86).

INGREDIENTS

50g (2 oz) unsalted butter
1 tablespoon olive oil
1 onion, peeled and diced
1 large carrot, peeled and diced
1 teaspoon dried mixed herbs
400g (14 oz) lean minced beef
120ml (4 fl. oz) whole milk
2 x 400g (14 oz) tins chopped tomatoes
Pinch of nutmeg
300g (10 oz) spaghetti
Freshly grated Cheddar or Parmesan cheese, to serve

- Make the Bolognese sauce. Heat the butter and oil in a large saucepan with a lid, over a low heat. Add the onion, carrot and dried herbs, and sauté for about 8–10 minutes, until softened but not browned. Add the minced beef and cook for about 6 minutes, stirring with a wooden spoon to break it up, until browned.

- Add the milk, tomatoes and nutmeg. Bring to the boil, then turn the heat down and simmer with the lid on for 40 minutes. The sauce will be quite juicy so take the lid off and cook for a further 15 minutes, allowing some of the liquid to evaporate.

- Cook the spaghetti according to the directions on the packet and serve with the Bolognese sauce and some Cheddar or Parmesan cheese grated on top.

 Keeps in the refrigerator for 2 days or in the freezer for 30 days.

- Purée or mash to the appropriate consistency for your baby or cut into small pieces for your toddler.

Family Dishes

THERE ONCE WAS A YOUNG GIRL CALLED SONIA
WHO MADE THE BEST SAUCE IN BOLOGNA
SO FULL OF MEAT AND VEG
IT BRIMMED OVER THE EDGE
AND ALL THOSE WHO ATE IT GREW STRONGER

All the Stage 2 recipes in the previous chapter are also appropriate for toddlers, older children and, in some cases, the whole family. However, they are basic and, most importantly, appropriate for the second stage of weaning. Once your baby becomes a toddler, it becomes easier to make a variety of meals the whole family will enjoy, although you should still watch salt and sugar levels.

I don't add any salt or sugar to these family dishes. Most use herbs and spices and all taste great without added salt (or sugar, which is an added ingredient in more savoury dishes than you might think). For adults and older children, it is certainly fine to season to taste.

Finding time to cook

When you have young children, it can be difficult to find the time to cook fresh, healthy meals day in and day out. In this cookbook we have accounted for shortage of time. There are dishes that take only minutes to prepare before you can put them in the oven, and many that can be made a day ahead, such as when the children have gone to bed, and left in the refrigerator overnight in preparation for the next day.

When my baby and toddler are both awake I find there is very little down time. I tend to use the simplest recipes (one-tomato ranking) when I want to put together something quickly and the recipes with two or three 'tomatoes' when they are napping.

Most dishes in this book can be frozen. It can be very useful to have some options in the freezer for those days when you are running short of time. Simply double a recipe and freeze half so you have a full meal on hand when you need it.

Dealing with fussy eaters

I don't know one mother who hasn't heard the words "I don't like it" at some point, especially during the toddler years. I find it frustrating when my three-year-old, Monty, tells me he doesn't like something before he's even tried it. Sometimes just the mention of something unfamiliar will result in a battle: "No, Mummy, I want pasta!"

Dealing with fussy eaters requires a huge amount of patience. We all know there are hectic nights when serving a favourite recipe will make mealtimes run more smoothly, but it's important to encourage toddlers to try new foods. You'll often find they like it once they've been persuaded to have a taste. When you encounter a great deal of resistance or your child refuses to eat their meal, it's generally best not to make too much of a fuss. Simply reinforce that in order to have anything else (fruit, yoghurt or a special treat), they must eat their main course. If they still won't eat, I find it's best to simply clear away the meal and let them get down from the table. In the effort to make the next meal a bit more success-ful, I don't offer snacks in between.

Comparing something new to a similar, familiar favourite can be a good way to encourage the first bite. For instance, one of Monty's favourites is Best Lasagne (page 94). When I first made him Chicken Enchiladas (page 76), I described it

as 'Mexican lasagne', which piqued his interest. After one bite, the struggle was over.

Getting the kids involved in cooking

Cooking with your children is a lovely way to spend time with them, not to mention a great activity when you need to keep them occupied.

Monty loves to cook. Even before he started walking, he loved playing with pots, pans and a wooden spoon. As he got older he started asking for things from the cupboard to put in his pots. Now he has his own little box of dried pasta, which he loves to open and pour from, filling one pan then another, mixing along the way.

We started cooking together when he was about 18 months old, using simple recipes like Fresh Fruit Muffins (page 130) and Banana Cupcakes (page 140). I was amazed that even at such a young age he had so much fun pouring in the ingredients, mixing everything up and waiting impatiently for the result to emerge from the oven. The very best part, of course, was the tasting.

As we expanded our repertoire, I realised that he likes making all kinds of recipes, not just treats. Better still, when he was involved in the preparation of the dish, he was more inclined to want to eat it.

In the recipes which follow we've indicated which steps are perfect for little hands when you want to get the children involved.

FAMILY DISHES

Fish

Easy Fish in Foil

SIMPLICITY:

SERVES:
4 small
or 2 older children

PREP TIME:
5 minutes

COOKING TIME:
12–15 minutes

My mother gave me this recipe and I use it all the time. It's super-easy and doesn't leave your kitchen smelling like fish. You can prepare ahead and leave the parcel of foil in the fridge for up to two days (as long as it's within its use-by date). Just take it out 15–20 minutes before cooking. It's easy to double or triple the quantity if you are feeding the whole family or a large group.

⭐ Leftovers will keep for 1–2 days in the refrigerator.

INGREDIENTS
2 x 150g (5 oz) salmon fillets (haddock, cod and halibut also work)
Dash of olive oil
1 garlic clove, crushed
Pinch of chopped fresh herbs
Squeeze of lemon

- Preheat the oven to 220°C/425°F/Gas 7.

- Take 2 large pieces of foil and place one on top of the other. (Using two pieces helps ensure there are no leaks.) Pour a small amount of oil on the top layer and brush across the surface. Check the fish fillets carefully for bones, then give them a quick rinse with cold water, pat dry and place side by side on the foil, skin-side down. Pour some more oil over the salmon (about 1 ¹/₂ tablespoons) and rub in.

- Sprinkle the salmon with the crushed garlic and the herbs of your choice and then squeeze some lemon juice over the top.

- Close the foil, leaving a little air in the parcel, and place the parcel on a baking tray. Bake for 12–15 minutes, being careful not to overcook. To test, open the parcel after 12 minutes and check whether the fish looks opaque all through: if it does, it is done. If not, reseal the parcel and continue to cook for another 2–3 minutes.

As an alternative to garlic and lemon, pour 2 tablespoons of soy or teriyaki sauce over the fish in addition to the olive oil.

Baked Cod

SIMPLICITY:

SERVES:
6–8 children or
a family of 4

PREP TIME:
5–10 minutes

COOKING TIME:
25 minutes

A very easy fish recipe when you are in a rush. The cheese is a nice finishing touch and especially appealing to kids when it comes out of the oven melted and bubbling. Grated mozzarella works best, but if you don't have any on hand, it's fine to use Cheddar instead. This recipe is easily halved.

INGREDIENTS

4 x 150g (5 oz) cod fillets
Knob of unsalted butter, melted
1 tablespoon lemon juice
1 garlic clove, crushed
400g (14 oz) chopped tomatoes (1 tin)
Freshly ground black pepper
60g (2 $\frac{1}{2}$ oz) mozzarella, grated

- Preheat the oven to 200°C/400°F/Gas 6.

- Check the cod for bones, using your fingers to feel for them. Give the cod a quick rinse under cold water, pat dry, then lay the fillets side by side in a lightly oiled baking dish, skin-side down.

- Combine the butter, lemon juice, garlic, chopped tomatoes and black pepper to taste. Pour the mixture over the fish. Sprinkle the grated cheese on top and bake for about 25 minutes, until the fish is cooked through and the cheese is bubbling and golden brown. Test the fish by inserting the tip of a knife into the flesh. When done, it will have lost its transparency and look opaque.

Serve with pasta, rice or couscous and a green vegetable

Monty's Favourite Fish Fingers

SIMPLICITY:

SERVES:
4 small or
2 older children

PREP TIME:
10 minutes

COOKING TIME:
5 minutes

This recipe is from my friend Alex. She makes these amazingly good fish fingers when we go round for play dates, and my son Monty loves them.

INGREDIENTS

2 x 150g (5 oz) lemon sole fillets (or haddock)
100ml (3 ¹/₂ fl. oz) whole milk
100g (3 ¹/₂ oz) plain flour
¹/₂ teaspoon freshly ground black pepper
Knob of unsalted butter
1 tablespoon olive oil

If your kids love dipping, serve these fish fingers with Simple Tomato Sauce (page 107) or crème fraiche mixed with a squeeze of lemon.

• Briefly rinse the fish fillets under cold water and pat dry. Pour the milk into a shallow bowl. Mix the flour and pepper together in a second shallow bowl. Dip each fillet into the milk, then coat in the seasoned flour.

• Heat the butter and olive oil in a frying pan on a medium heat and sauté the fillets for a couple of minutes on each side, until the fish is no longer translucent in the centre. Cut into strips and serve immediately.

Salmon and Pesto

I find most kids love pesto, especially if you introduce it with pasta first. This recipe is a great way to encourage your children to eat salmon, an important source of Omega 3 which is beneficial for brain development. Simply halve the ingredients if you are feeding a smaller group.

INGREDIENTS
4 x 125g (4 ½ oz) salmon fillets
145g tub (about 5 oz) fresh basil pesto
1-2 tablespoons lemon juice, to taste
40g (1 ½ oz) fresh breadcrumbs (1 slice brown bread)

• Preheat the oven to 200°C/400°F/Gas 6.

• Check the salmon carefully for bones, using your fingers to feel for them. Give the salmon a quick rinse under cold water, pat dry, then lay the fillets side by side in a lightly oiled baking dish, skin-side down.

• Combine the pesto, lemon juice, and breadcrumbs in a small bowl, then spread over the salmon. Bake for about 15 minutes or until the salmon is cooked through. Test by inserting the tip of a knife into the flesh. When done, it will have lost its transparency and look opaque all through.

SERVES:
6-8 children or
a family of 4

PREP TIME:
5 minutes

COOKING TIME:
15 minutes

Fresh breadcrumbs are easily made with a grater or hand blender.

Serve with rice, couscous or pasta and a green vegetable.

Fishcakes

These take some time to prepare but are delicious to eat and fun to make, too. Children love to help with mixing the ingredients and forming the fishcakes.

SIMPLICITY:

SERVES:
8 children or
a family of 4 with
leftovers

PREP TIME:
25 minutes

COOKING TIME:
12–15 minutes

⭐ Cooked fishcakes keep in the refrigerator for 2 days or in the freezer for 30 days.

INGREDIENTS

2 x 125g (4 ¹/₂ oz) pieces cod, skin removed

2 x 125g (4 ¹/₂ oz) pieces salmon, skin removed

2 potatoes, peeled and quartered

40g (1 ¹/₂ oz) unsalted butter

1 small onion, peeled and finely chopped

1 garlic clove, crushed

1 egg yolk and 1 whole egg

1 tablespoon chopped fresh flat-leaf parsley

2 teaspoons lemon juice

50g (2 oz) flour seasoned with ¹/₄ teaspoon freshly ground black pepper

1 egg, beaten

100g (3 ¹/₂ oz) fresh breadcrumbs (2 ¹/₂ slices of brown bread)

Butter and olive oil, to sauté

- Preheat the oven to 200°C/400°F/Gas 6.

- Check the fish carefully for bones, then rinse in cold water and pat dry. Bake the cod and salmon in foil with a bit of olive oil for 12–14 minutes or until the fish is cooked through (see the method for Easy Fish in Foil on page 50). Take the fish from the parcel, flake the flesh and set aside. Discard the skin.

- Meanwhile, boil the potatoes for about 20 minutes, until tender. Drain, allow to steam briefly in the warm pan then mash with half of the butter. Set aside.

- Melt the remaining butter in a saucepan and add the onion and garlic. Cook for 4–5 minutes, until soft, then transfer to a mixing bowl and add the mashed potato, flaked fish, egg yolk, parsley and lemon juice. Mix together well.

- Divide the mixture into 8–10 pieces and shape each one into a fishcake. Put the seasoned flour into one shallow dish, the beaten egg into another and the breadcrumb mixture into a third. Coat each fishcake first in the flour, then the egg, then the breadcrumbs.

- Melt the oil with the butter in a pan over medium heat. Cook the fishcakes for about 8–10 minutes, until golden brown on both sides and warmed right through to the middle. Serve immediately.

The fishcakes can be made ahead and chilled in the refrigerator for an hour or so before cooking. Serve with steamed vegetables or Broccoli, Leek and Cauliflower Bake (page 124).

Fish Pie

SIMPLICITY:

SERVES:
6 children or a
family of 4

PREP TIME:
20–25 minutes

COOKING TIME:
25 minutes

This dish is not as quick as others in the book, but it is a crowd pleaser for the whole family and you don't need to prepare any side dishes as it is a healthy, wholesome meal on its own.

INGREDIENTS
2 x 150g (5 oz) cod fillets
250ml (9 fl. oz) milk for poaching
5 medium potatoes, peeled and quartered
Knob of butter and dash of milk, for mashing
100g (3 ½ oz) broccoli florets
3 medium carrots, peeled and roughly chopped

For the cheese sauce:
30g (1 oz) unsalted butter
30g (1 oz) plain flour
400ml (³/₄ pint) whole milk
90g (3 oz) Cheddar cheese, grated

- Preheat the oven to 180°C/350°F/Gas 4.

- Check the cod for bones, using your fingers to feel for them.
  Give the cod a quick rinse under cold water, pat dry, then
  place in a saucepan and pour the milk over. Poach over a
  low heat for 10-12 minutes. Drain, flake with a fork and set
  aside. Discard the skin.

- While the fish is cooking, boil the potatoes for about 15
  minutes or until tender, then drain and mash with a little
  milk and butter. Steam the broccoli for 3-5 minutes and the
  carrots for 10 minutes and chop both finely. Set aside.

- Meanwhile, make the cheese sauce. Melt the butter in a
  saucepan over medium heat and whisk in the flour until
  smooth. Slowly whisk in the milk, stirring the whole time
  so it doesn't become lumpy. When all the milk has been
  added, bring to the boil then turn the heat down and
  simmer, continuing to stir until thick enough to coat the
  spoon or whisk. Add most of the Cheddar cheese (reserving
  a little for the topping), and stir for a further 3 minutes until
  the cheese has melted and the sauce is thick and smooth.

- Assemble the pie in a casserole dish: first the fish in a layer,
  then the broccoli and carrots, then the cheese sauce. Spoon
  the mashed potato on top and sprinkle with the reserved
  Cheddar cheese. Bake for around 25 minutes, until the
  cheese is bubbling and golden brown.

An alternative to poaching is to bake the fish in foil at 200°C/ 400°F/Gas 6 for 12-15 minutes.

Leftovers can be frozen for 30 days.

Poultry

Simple Roast Chicken

SERVES:
family of 4 with
leftovers

PREP TIME:
5 minutes

COOKING TIME:
45-90 minutes

The perfect recipe for a cosy Sunday lunch,
but easy enough for a weeknight dinner too.

INGREDIENTS

1 whole chicken

2 onions

1 lemon

5 sprigs of fresh thyme or rosemary (optional)

1 whole garlic bulb

3 tablespoons olive oil

Freshly ground black pepper

- Preheat the oven to 180°C/350°F/Gas 4. Weigh the chicken so you can calculate the cooking time.

- Remove the giblets from the chicken if there are any. Give the chicken a rinse under cold water and pat dry. Peel and halve one onion and halve the lemon; put the onion and lemon halves inside the chicken along with 2–3 sprigs of fresh herbs, if using.

- Slice the other onion (with skin on) and separate the garlic cloves. Scatter the onion slices and garlic cloves (with skin on) over the base of a baking tray and place the chicken on top. Spoon the olive oil over the skin and rub it in well. Strip the leaves from the remaining sprigs of herbs and sprinkle over the chicken, along with some black pepper.

- Place the baking tray in the oven and roast the chicken for about 40 minutes per kilo (18 minutes per pound), until cooked.

- Let the chicken rest for 15–20 minutes before carving and serving.

Chicken Pasta Bake

SIMPLICITY:

SERVES:
6 children or a
family of 4

PREP TIME:
25 minutes

COOKING TIME:
15 minutes

A tasty, healthy dish which is a good use of left-over roast chicken (or turkey after the Christmas holiday). If you're not using leftovers, simply bake two chicken breasts in the oven while you're cooking the broccoli and pasta. My family likes Gruyère cheese best in this recipe, but you can easily substitute Cheddar instead.

INGREDIENTS

2 x 150g (5 oz) cooked skinless chicken breasts
200g (7 oz) broccoli, chopped into florets
200g (7 oz) short pasta, such as penne or fusilli
Knob of unsalted butter
100g (3½ oz) mushrooms, finely chopped
1 garlic clove, crushed
1–2 teaspoons dried mixed herbs
25g (1 oz) plain flour
360ml (12 fl. oz) chicken stock (page 30) or shop-bought
  with no added salt
120ml (4 fl. oz) whole milk
60g (2 oz) Gruyère cheese, grated
Freshly ground black pepper
40g (1 ½ oz) fresh breadcrumbs (1 slice of brown bread)
2 tablespoons freshly grated Parmesan cheese

- Preheat the oven to 220°C/425°F/Gas 7.

- Dice the cooked chicken breasts and set aside.

- Cook the broccoli in boiling water for 5 minutes; remove the broccoli using a slotted spoon and set aside. Return the water to the boil and cook the pasta for 10–12 minutes or according to the directions on the packet. Drain and set aside.

- Meanwhile, melt the butter in a large saucepan over a medium heat; add the mushrooms, garlic and herbs and sauté for 4 minutes. Add the flour before gradually adding the chicken stock and milk; give it a good stir with a whisk. Bring to the boil and cook for 5 minutes, until thick, stirring from time to time. Add the Gruyère, a pinch of pepper and stir well. Take the pan off the heat and stir in the cooked diced chicken.

- Grease a casserole dish and put a layer of pasta on the bottom, roughly half. Put half the broccoli on top, followed by half the chicken mixture, then repeat with a second layer of each. Sprinkle the top with the breadcrumbs and grated Parmesan and bake for 15 minutes, until bubbling and golden brown.

Spaghetti or tagliatelle works well in this dish if you are making it for older children or adults. Simply substitute 200g of long pasta for the short pasta.

Leftovers can be frozen for 30 days.

Caruso's Chicken

SIMPLICITY:

SERVES:
6 children or a
family of 4

PREP TIME:
5 minutes, plus
30 minutes–24 hours
marinating

COOKING TIME:
10–15 minutes

Caruso's is an authentic Italian delicatessen on the waterfront near where my mother lives in Long Island. Everything they make is delicious, but Monty especially fell in love with their grilled chicken. They were kind enough to share the recipe with me, which you'll see is very simple. You can omit the wine, but the flavour is much better with it, and you don't have to worry about the alcohol content as it is only used as a marinade.

INGREDIENTS
4 boneless skinless chicken breasts
Juice of 1 lemon
2 garlic cloves, crushed
3 tablespoons white wine
3 tablespoons extra virgin olive oil

- Rinse the chicken and pat dry. Place each chicken breast one at a time in a bag or on a large chopping board and pound to make it as thin as possible.

- Marinate the pounded chicken in the lemon juice, garlic, white wine and olive oil in the refrigerator for at least 30 minutes or ideally overnight.

- Preheat the grill to medium-hot. Take the chicken from the marinade and grill for 10–15 minutes, until cooked, turning over halfway through. Slice the chicken and serve hot or at room temperature.

Excellent with Marta's Rice & Peas (page 112) or Broccoli, Leek and Cauliflower Bake (page 124). Leftovers are great for sandwiches.

Marinated Chicken with Broccoli Trees

SIMPLICITY:

SERVES:
6 children or a
family of 4

PREP TIME:
5-10 minutes, plus
2-24 hours marinating

COOKING TIME:
25-30 minutes

The marinade in this dish is so tasty, it's usually easy to convince children to eat their 'broccoli trees'.

INGREDIENTS

4 x 150g (5 oz) boneless skinless chicken breasts
200g (7 oz) broccoli
1 garlic clove, crushed
3 tablespoons soy sauce
1 tablespoon honey
Juice of 1 lime
2 tablespoons sunflower or rapeseed oil

- Rinse the chicken and pat dry. Cut each chicken breast lengthways into 3–4 strips and put in an ovenproof dish. Chop the broccoli into florets ('trees') and add to the chicken.

- Mix together the crushed garlic, soy sauce, honey, lime juice and sunflower or rapeseed oil, then pour over the chicken and broccoli. Leave to marinate in the refrigerator for at least 2 hours or overnight.

- Preheat the oven to 200°C/400°F/Gas 6.

- Bring the marinated chicken back to room temperature, then bake in the oven for 25–30 minutes, until cooked through. Stir or baste halfway through so the broccoli does not dry out.

If you are in a hurry, it's fine to skip the marinating stage, but the chicken will be especially moist and flavourful if you have the time. Serve with rice or noodles.

Chicken Milanese

SIMPLICITY:

SERVES:
4 children

PREP TIME:
10-15 minutes

COOKING TIME:
10 minutes

Marta is from Portugal and an amazing cook. She gave us this recipe, which is a huge hit with kids, and better than any other chicken finger recipe we tried. Double the recipe if you're feeding a family of four or if you want to freeze leftovers for another time.

INGREDIENTS

2 x 150g (5 oz) boneless skinless chicken breasts
160g (6 oz) fresh breadcrumbs (4 slices of brown bread)
2 tablespoons finely chopped fresh flat-leaf parsley
1 garlic clove, crushed
Freshly ground black pepper
1 egg
2-3 tablespoons sunflower oil or olive oil

- Rinse the chicken breasts and pat dry. Place each chicken breast one at a time in a bag or on a large chopping board and pound to make it as thin as possible.

- In a shallow bowl, combine the breadcrumbs, parsley, crushed garlic and a grinding of black pepper. Break the egg into a separate shallow bowl and beat it.

- Dip each chicken breast in the egg, then the breadcrumb mixture.

- Heat the sunflower oil or olive oil in a frying pan and sauté the chicken on both sides until golden and cooked through, about 5 minutes on each side. Place the cooked chicken on some kitchen paper to absorb any excess oil. Cut into 'chicken bites' and serve hot or at room temperature.

For another great dish, simply cover the chicken bites with Simple Tomato Sauce (page 107) and a sprinkling of grated mozzarella cheese. Bake at 180°C/350°F/ Gas 4 until the cheese is bubbling and golden-brown.

These keep brilliantly: just wrap the uncooked bread-crumbed breasts in clingfilm and freeze them. To cook, thaw completely in the refrigerator, then sauté as above.

Chicken Pie

SIMPLICITY:

SERVES:
8 children or family
of 4 with leftovers

PREP TIME:
30 minutes

COOKING TIME:
30-40 minutes

This is a staple in our household. Monty loves it, as does his baby brother Ridley, for whom I simply mash the pie well with a fork. It's relatively straightforward the first time you make it and once you've done it a few times you won't even need to refer to the recipe. It looks impressive when it comes out of the oven and your kitchen will have the lovely scent of home-baked chicken pie.

INGREDIENTS

4 x 150g (5 oz) boneless skinless chicken breasts
480ml (17 fl. oz) chicken stock (page 30) or shop-bought
 with no added salt
1 tablespoon olive oil
1 large onion, peeled and finely chopped
1 leek, thinly sliced
2 carrots, peeled and chopped
60g (generous 2 oz) unsalted butter
60g (generous 2 oz) plain flour
360ml (12 fl. oz) whole milk
1-2 teaspoons dried thyme or mixed herbs
125g (4 ½ oz) frozen peas, thawed
2 tablespoons roughly chopped fresh flat-leaf parsley
1 sheet of puff pastry

- Preheat the oven to 200°C/400°F/Gas 6.

- Rinse the chicken under cold water. Put the chicken and stock into a saucepan over medium heat. Cover and bring to the boil, then turn the down and simmer for 8-10 minutes, until chicken is cooked through. Transfer the chicken to a separate bowl, reserving the liquid in a measuring jug to add to the sauce later.

- Heat the oil in the same pan, add the onion, leek and carrots and sauté for about 8 minutes, until soft. While the vegetables are cooking, cut the chicken into small pieces and put it into the bowl. When the vegetables are ready, add them to the bowl.

- Over low heat, melt the butter in the same pan. Add the flour, stir well and cook for 1 minute. Gradually whisk in the reserved chicken stock, milk and thyme. Bring to the boil, then turn the heat down and simmer for another 2 minutes, stirring constantly, until the sauce thickens enough to coat the spoon. Add the chicken and vegetables and stir in the peas and parsley.

- Pour the chicken mixture into a 32 x 22cm (13 x 8 ½ in) baking dish. Lay the pastry sheet over the top, stretching a bit if necessary. Trim the pastry to fit the baking dish, crimping the edges, and cut a few slits to vent the steam. Place the dish on a baking sheet and bake for 30-40 minutes until the crust is golden and the filling is bubbling.

When my husband makes this recipe he adds 100g (3 ½ oz) diced pancetta when sautéing the vegetables for extra flavour.

Leftovers can be frozen for 30 days. Reheat from frozen in the oven (at 180°C/350°F/Gas 4) or in the microwave.

Creamy Chicken Curry

A lovely mild dish, perfect for introducing curry to young children. Simply increase the amount of red chillies to add more spice for older palates.

Serve with basmati rice and naan bread. Blend the leftover coconut milk with bananas for a tasty smoothie dessert.

INGREDIENTS

4 x 150g (5 oz) boneless skinless chicken breasts

150ml (5 fl. oz) natural yoghurt

1 garlic clove, crushed

A thumb-sized piece of ginger, grated

1/2-1 fresh red chilli, finely chopped

30g (just over 1 oz) unsalted butter

2 medium onions, peeled and diced

1 teaspoon ground cumin

1 teaspoon ground coriander

1/2 teaspoon turmeric

150ml (5 fl. oz) coconut milk

3 large ripe tomatoes, peeled and chopped

1/2 tablespoon chopped fresh coriander

- Rinse the chicken, pat dry and chop into bite-size pieces. Mix the yoghurt, garlic, ginger and chilli in a bowl and add the chicken. Leave to marinate for 6 hours or overnight.

- Preheat the oven to 220°C/425°F/Gas 7.

- Melt the butter in a saucepan over medium heat, add the onions and cook for a few minutes until they begin to soften. Add the ground cumin, coriander and turmeric and cook for 2–3 minutes. Add the coconut milk, and continue cooking until the onions are completely soft. Take the pan off the heat and purée the mixture using a hand blender.

- Meanwhile, place the chicken on a baking tray and roast for 10–15 minutes, until browned. When ready, drain off any liquid and stir into the blended coconut milk and onion mixture, along with the tomatoes. Return the pan to the heat and warm through. Stir in the fresh coriander just before serving.

Chicken Enchiladas

My friend Jane gave me this recipe. It is delicious comfort food and kids love it. I added the spinach and red pepper, but you could easily leave those out. You can make this in advance and leave it in the refrigerator for up to 24 hours before cooking.

INGREDIENTS

4 x 150g (5 oz) boneless skinless chicken breasts

50g (2 oz) unsalted butter

50g (2 oz) plain flour

300ml (10 fl. oz) chicken stock (page 30) or shop-bought with no added salt

120ml (4 fl. oz) water, plus extra for poaching

150ml (5 fl. oz) soured cream

1 $\frac{1}{2}$ green chillies, deseeded and finely chopped (optional)

6 spring onions, chopped

200g (7 oz) Cheddar cheese, grated

8 soft flour tortillas

1 red or yellow pepper, thinly sliced

150–200g (5–7 oz) fresh spinach leaves

SIMPLICITY:

SERVES:
8 children or
a family of 6

PREP TIME:
30–35 minutes

COOKING TIME:
15 minutes

Leave out the spring onions if your children resist 'bits'. This dish is great with green salad and guacamole.

- Preheat the oven to 200°C/400°F/Gas 6.

- Rinse the chicken breasts and pat dry. Put some water in a saucepan that is wide enough for the chicken breasts to sit in a single layer. Bring to the boil, then turn the heat down to a simmer before adding the chicken breasts. Poach for 10-12 minutes, until chicken is cooked through. Remove the chicken breasts and set aside.

- Melt the butter in a saucepan over medium heat and whisk in the flour until smooth. Slowly whisk in the chicken stock and water, then cook, stirring well, until the sauce has thickened enough to coat the spoon or whisk.

- Take off the heat and stir in the soured cream and green chillies. Spread half the sauce on the bottom of a 22 x 28 cm (8 ½ x 11 in) ovenproof dish and set the other half aside.

- Shred the poached chicken into a bowl and mix in the chopped spring onions and half the grated cheese.

- Fill tortillas as follows: add chicken mixture, a few slices of pepper and a handful of spinach. Roll each tortilla and line up in the ovenproof dish, seam-side down, then pour the rest of the sauce on top. Top with the remaining Cheddar cheese and bake for 15 minutes.

This recipe is easily doubled for a large group. Or freeze a portion after the enchiladas have been assembled but not yet baked. To cook from frozen, bake at 180°C/ 350°F/ Gas 4 for 30 minutes.

GG's Chicken Supreme

SIMPLICITY:

SERVES:
6 children or a
family of 4

PREP TIME:
10 minutes,
plus 24 hours
marinating

COOKING TIME:
45 minutes

This is one of my mother's great 'make ahead' recipes: you throw the chicken and marinade together, keep in the refrigerator overnight and then bake the following day. The result is a really moist chicken dish that kids love but is also good enough to serve at an adult dinner party with some nice side dishes.

INGREDIENTS

4 x 150g (5 oz) boneless skinless chicken breasts

150ml (5 fl. oz) soured cream

1 tablespoon lemon juice

1 garlic clove, crushed

1 tablespoon Worcestershire sauce

1 teaspoon paprika

Pinch of freshly ground black pepper

250g (9 oz) fresh breadcrumbs (6 slices of brown bread)

1 tablespoon freshly grated Parmesan cheese

90g (3 oz) unsalted butter, melted

- Rinse the chicken breasts and pat dry. In a large mixing bowl, combine the soured cream, lemon juice, garlic and seasonings. Add the chicken breasts, coating each one well, then cover the bowl and leave to marinate overnight in the refrigerator.

- The next day, preheat the oven to 180°C/350°F/Gas 4.

- Combine the breadcrumbs and Parmesan cheese in a shallow dish. Take each chicken breast, still coated in the soured-cream marinade, and press firmly on both sides into the breadcrumb mixture. Arrange in a single layer in a greased baking tray and drizzle the melted butter evenly over the top.

- Bake uncovered for 45 minutes, until the chicken is cooked through and the breadcrumbs are golden and crisp.

Add a pinch of celery salt to the soured-cream mixture if you are making the dish for older children or adults. Serve with Ratatouille Bake (page 114) or Green Pie (page 118).

Turkey Meatballs

SIMPLICITY:

SERVES:
6 children or
a family of 4

PREP TIME:
10 minutes

COOKING TIME:
10-15 minutes

I have yet to meet a child who doesn't like meatballs. This recipe is a nice change from red meat, although beef or lamb mince can be substituted for the turkey. These are very good served with pasta and tomato sauce, or with mashed potato and a green vegetable.

INGREDIENTS
500g (1lb) minced turkey
80g (3 oz) fresh breadcrumbs (2 slices of brown bread)
1 small onion, peeled and grated
1 egg, beaten
50g (2 oz) freshly grated Parmesan or Cheddar cheese
1 teaspoon dried mixed herbs
2 teaspoons olive oil

- Combine all the ingredients, except the olive oil, by hand in a mixing bowl. If the mixture feels too wet, add more bread-crumbs.

- Roll into small balls. You should be able to make between 20 and 25 meatballs.

- Add the olive oil to a pan with a lid. Cook the meatballs for 6 minutes on each side with the lid on, until cooked through. You may need to cook the meatballs in two batches.

Combining and shaping meatballs or burgers is a great job for small hands who want to help out.

Turkey Burgers

This recipe is from my friend Patty, and it proved to be a huge hit in our household. She uses single cream, which I didn't have on hand the first time I made it, so I substituted whole milk. Both work well.

INGREDIENTS
80g (3 oz) fresh breadcrumbs (2 slices of brown bread)
75ml (2 ¹/₂ fl. oz) whole milk
500g (1lb) minced turkey
¹/₂ teaspoon freshly ground black pepper
Pinch of nutmeg
1 tablespoon chopped fresh flat-leaf parsley
Knob of unsalted butter

- Combine all the ingredients, except the butter, by hand in a bowl. Divide and shape into 8 mini-burgers or 4 larger burgers. Let them stand for 15 minutes.

- Heat the butter in a saucepan until it bubbles and starts to brown. Add the burgers and cook until brown and crisp on both sides and cooked through.

SIMPLICITY:

SERVES:
8 children
or a family of 4

PREP TIME:
20 minutes (includes 15 minutes' standing time)

COOKING TIME:
8–12 minutes

 For a citrus twist, add 4 teaspoons freshly grated lemon zest (about 1 ¹/₂ lemons) to the turkey mixture before making into burgers.

Meat

Simple Lamb Hotpot

SIMPLICITY:

SERVES:
8 children or
a family of 6

PREP TIME:
10 minutes

COOKING TIME:
2–2 ½ hours

This recipe can be assembled in a very short time, especially as you do not need to brown the meat. But do plan ahead because it needs a couple of hours in the oven.

INGREDIENTS

700g (1lb 9 oz) lamb shoulder or neck fillet, trimmed of fat and cut into bite-size pieces

3 large red potatoes (500g or 1lb), peeled and sliced into ½ cm rounds

1 medium onion, peeled and sliced into rounds

Freshly ground black pepper

1–2 sprigs of fresh thyme, leaves stripped

360ml (12 fl. oz) beef stock with no added salt

- Preheat the oven to 170°C/325°F/Gas 3.

- In a casserole dish, arrange the lamb, potatoes and onion in layers, seasoning each layer with freshly ground pepper. Finish with a top layer of potatoes. Sprinkle the fresh thyme leaves on top and pour in the stock.

- Put the lid on the casserole and cook in the oven for 2–2 ½ hours, until the meat is tender and the sauce is thickened. Remove lid for final 15 minutes of cooking time to ensure the top is nicely browned.

Serve with some steamed vegetables and crusty bread. Add 300ml (10 fl. oz) red wine for a richer stew for adults or older children.

Proper Bolognese

Don't let the cooking time needed for this recipe put you off. It is very straightforward and once you've added all the ingredients, just leave to gently simmer for a few hours. It tastes even better the next day.

INGREDIENTS

2 tablespoons olive oil

2 garlic cloves, crushed

1 onion, peeled and finely sliced

1 carrot, peeled and diced

1 tablespoon dried mixed herbs

500g (1lb) lean minced beef

100g (3 ½ oz) mushrooms, diced

240ml (8 ½ fl. oz) whole milk

240ml (8 ½ fl. oz) white wine

2 x 400g (14 oz) tins chopped tomatoes

Freshly ground black pepper

Spaghetti, tagliatelle or other pasta, to serve (cooked according to packet directions)

Freshly grated Parmesan cheese, to serve

- Melt the olive oil in a large, heavy-bottomed pot over a medium heat. Add the garlic, onion, carrot, and mixed herbs and sauté for about 6 minutes, until softened but not browned.

- Add the minced meat, crumbling it with the edge of a wooden spoon. Cook for about 5-6 minutes, continuing to crumble the meat, until it loses its raw colour but has not yet browned. Add the mushrooms and stir well.

- Add the milk and bring to the boil, then turn the heat down and simmer for 10-15 minutes, until the milk evaporates and only clear fat remains. Add the wine and simmer for a further 10-15 minutes, until the wine evaporates.

- Add the tomatoes and their juice and bring back to the boil. Reduce the heat to low so the sauce continues to simmer just barely, with an occasional bubble or two at the surface, for about 3 hours, until the liquid has evaporated. Season with black pepper to taste.

- Serve with cooked pasta and sprinkle with freshly grated Parmesan cheese.

If doubling this recipe, increase simmering times for milk and wine to 30 minutes each and once the tomatoes are added to 4 hours. This sauce can be frozen for 60 days.

Hearty Beef Stew

SIMPLICITY:

SERVES:
6 children or a family
of 4 with leftovers

PREP TIME:
25-30 minutes

COOKING TIME:
1 hour 30 minutes

Good with crusty
bread and a green
salad.

This is a relatively simple but tasty stew. My whole family loves it, and I even puréed it down for my youngest son, Ridley, when he was eating baby food.

INGREDIENTS

20g (³/₄ oz) unsalted butter

2 tablespoons olive oil

1 onion, peeled and sliced

2 garlic cloves, crushed

1 carrot, peeled and diced

1 potato, peeled and diced

1 sweet potato, peeled and diced

450g (1lb) stewing beef, cut into 1 ¹/₂ cm (¹/₂ in) cubes

1 tablespoon plain flour, seasoned with freshly ground
  black pepper

300ml (10 fl. oz) beef stock with no added salt

1 tablespoon tomato purée

1 tablespoon fresh thyme leaves

1 bay leaf

2 tablespoons chopped fresh flat-leaf parsley

- Preheat the oven to 150°C/300°F/Gas 2.

- Melt half the butter and olive oil in a frying pan over a medium-high heat, add the onion and garlic and allow the onion to brown a little. Then add the carrot, potato and sweet potato and stir to coat in the oil, before transferring to a casserole dish.

- Rinse the beef and pat dry. Coat the beef in the seasoned flour. Turn the heat up under the frying pan very slightly, add the remaining butter and olive oil and cook the beef until lightly brown all over. Transfer to the casserole dish.

- Bring the stock to the boil in a saucepan, add the juices from the frying pan and the tomato purée and pour over the meat and vegetables in the casserole dish. Add the thyme and bay leaf. Cover and cook in the oven for 1 1/2 hours. Top with chopped parsley before serving.

Meatloaf

SIMPLICITY:

SERVES:
8 children or a family
of 6 with leftovers

PREP TIME:
15-20 minutes

COOKING TIME:
50 minutes

This is a fantastic, easy dish. You can make it ahead and keep it in the refrigerator for a few hours before cooking, just return to room temperature before baking. Kids love it straight from the oven or as sandwiches the next day. Or there's my husband's take, which on a Sunday involves a fried egg on top and a Bloody Mary.

INGREDIENTS

$\frac{1}{2}$ **small onion, peeled and diced**

1 large carrot, peeled and diced

2 eggs, beaten

60ml (2 fl. oz) whole milk

$\frac{1}{2}$ **tablespoon chopped fresh flat-leaf parsley**

1 tablespoon Worcestershire sauce

2 tablespoons freshly grated Parmesan cheese

$\frac{1}{4}$ **teaspoon freshly ground black pepper**

100g (3 $\frac{1}{2}$ oz) fresh breadcrumbs (2 $\frac{1}{2}$ slices of brown bread)

2 teaspoons Dijon mustard (optional)

500g (1lb) lean minced beef

500g (1lb) lean minced pork

- Preheat the oven to 190°C/375°F/Gas 5.

- Line a baking tray with foil. Lightly oil the foil.

- Combine all the ingredients, apart from the meat, in a large bowl and mix together thoroughly. Using your hands, add the minced beef and pork and make sure it is well mixed in and evenly distributed.

- Shape your ingredients into a loaf and place on the baking tray. The loaf should not touch the sides of the tray but sit nicely in the middle. Bake for 45-50 minutes, then let it stand for 10 minutes before serving.

If the meatloaf is to be on display, reposition it on a serving platter as the baking tray will look greasy when it comes out of the oven.

Chilli & Rice Bake

SIMPLICITY:

SERVES:
6 children or
family of 4

PREP TIME:
25 minutes

COOKING TIME:
10 minutes

This dish was extremely popular in our recipe-testing sessions. It can be eaten on its own or wrapped in flour tortillas. If your children will go for kidney beans, add a tin (drained) after the chopped tomatoes.

INGREDIENTS

250g (9 oz) long-grain rice

300g (10 oz) lean minced beef

2 small onions, chopped

1 green or red pepper, chopped

60ml (2 fl. oz) beef stock with no added salt

1–2 teaspoon chilli powder

2 teaspoons ground cumin

$^1/_2$ teaspoon dried oregano

1 x 400g (14 oz) tin chopped tomatoes

175ml (6 fl. oz) soured cream

60ml (2 fl. oz) semi-skimmed milk

120g (4 oz) Cheddar cheese, grated

- Preheat the oven to 190°C/375°F/Gas 5.

- Cook the rice according to the packet directions, drain and set aside for later.

- Cook the beef, onion and peppers over a medium heat in a saucepan with a lid, stirring until the meat is browned all over. Add the beef stock, chilli powder, cumin, oregano and chopped tomatoes and bring to the boil. Cover, turn the heat down and simmer for 10 minutes. Then take the lid off and cook for a further 2 minutes. Remove from the heat and set aside.

· Combine the rice, soured cream and milk in a bowl and then spoon into a 20 x 30cm (8 ¹/₂ x 11 ¹/₂ in) baking dish. Cover with the beef mixture and scatter the cheese over the top. Bake in the oven for 10 minutes, until heated through and the cheese is bubbling and golden.

The Best Lasagne

SIMPLICITY:

SERVES:
8 children or a family
of 4 with leftovers

PREP TIME:
30-40 minutes

COOKING TIME:
45-55 minutes

This recipe takes a bit longer than most in this book, but it's worth it. It's honestly one of the best lasagnes we've ever tasted and was such a hit with Monty that one of his first words was 'sagne (pronounced 'zanya'). The cheese sauce makes it yummy and appealing to kids, allowing you to sneak in that layer of spinach.

INGREDIENTS

2 tablespoons olive oil
2 medium onions, peeled and finely chopped
3 garlic cloves, crushed
500g (1lb) lean minced beef
2 tablespoons tomato purée
2 tablespoon dried mixed herbs
2 x 400g (14 oz) tins chopped tomatoes
60g (generous 2 oz) unsalted butter
60g (generous 2 oz) plain flour
1 litre (2 pints) whole milk
Pinch of nutmeg
125g (4 ½ oz) Cheddar cheese, grated
200g (7 oz) fresh spinach leaves
150g (5 oz) mozzarella cheese, grated
7-8 lasagne sheets
3 tablespoons freshly grated Parmesan cheese

- Preheat the oven to 180°C/350°F/Gas 4.

- Pour the olive oil into a large saucepan and place over a medium heat. Add the onions and garlic and sauté for about 3 minutes, then add the mince and cook, stirring, until brown all over. Stir in the tomato purée, herbs and the tinned tomatoes. Bring to the boil then turn the heat down and simmer for 30 minutes.

- Meanwhile, make the cheese sauce. Melt the butter in a saucepan over medium heat and whisk in the flour until smooth. Slowly whisk in the milk, stirring the whole time so it doesn't become lumpy. When all the milk has been added, bring to the boil, then turn the heat down to a simmer and continue to stir until thick enough to coat the spoon or whisk. Add the nutmeg and Cheddar cheese and stir for a further 3 minutes until the cheese has melted and the sauce is thick and smooth.

- Assemble the lasagne in a baking dish 32 x 22 cm (13 x 8 ½ in): begin with a layer of the meat, then add lasagne sheets (about 4), another layer of meat, a layer of spinach, half the cheese sauce and half the grated mozzarella. Add the rest of the lasagne sheets in another layer, then the rest of the meat, spinach, cheese sauce and the mozzarella. Sprinkle the grated Parmesan cheese on top and bake for 45–55 minutes.

The lasagne can be prepared a day ahead and kept in the refrigerator. Bring to room temperature before baking. Leftovers can be frozen for 30 days.

Burger with Hidden Vegetables

SIMPLICITY:

SERVES:
8 children or
a family of 4

PREP TIME:
10 minutes

COOKING TIME:
10–15 minutes

Nothing beats a good burger, and kids love them. My husband doctored up this recipe with finely chopped spinach, which mixes in unnoticed. This recipe is one of several in the book which requires mixing by hand, a job which small children are often more than willing to assist.

INGREDIENTS

Knob of unsalted butter
100g (3 ¹/₂ oz) spinach
500g (1lb) lean minced beef
¹/₂ onion, peeled and grated
2 egg yolks
Freshly ground black pepper
1–2 teaspoons Worcestershire sauce (to taste)

- Melt the butter in a frying pan and sauté the spinach for about 2 minutes, until wilted. Allow to cool, chop finely and put into a mixing bowl.

- Add the minced beef, onion and egg yolks to the spinach and mix well, using your hands. Season with a pinch of ground pepper and Worcestershire sauce.

- Divide into 4 or 8 pieces and form each into a burger. Heat a grill pan or frying pan over a high heat, then cook the burgers for 10–15 minutes, turning halfway through.

Serve on a whole-meal roll with salad.

Shepherd's Pie

SIMPLICITY:

SERVES:
6 children or
family of 4

PREP TIME:
30 minutes

COOKING TIME:
30 minutes

This recipe is a classic that never lets me down. It's not difficult to make, and even on its own with no side dishes it makes a properly balanced meal.

INGREDIENTS

4 large potatoes

100g (3 ½ oz) unsalted butter

1 onion, peeled and chopped

2 carrots, peeled and chopped

1 garlic clove, crushed

150g (5 oz) frozen peas, thawed

500g (1lb) lean minced lamb

150ml (5 fl. oz) beef stock with no added salt

1-2 tablespoons whole milk

- Preheat the oven to 200°C/400°F/Gas 6.

- Peel and quarter the potatoes, then boil for about 20 minutes, until tender.

- While the potatoes are cooking, melt 25g (1 oz) of the butter in a large pan and over a medium heat sauté the onions, carrots and garlic for about 10 minutes, until tender. Stir in the peas.

- Add the lamb mince and cook until no longer pink. Add half the beef stock and cook, uncovered, over a low heat for 10 minutes, adding more stock as necessary to keep it moist.

- Drain the potatoes and mash with the remaining butter and the milk. Place the lamb mixture in a baking dish. Layer the mashed potato on top. Rough up with a fork so there are peaks that will brown nicely.

- Bake in the oven for about 30 minutes, until bubbling and brown. Place under the grill for the last few minutes to brown if necessary.

Top with Cheddar cheese if your kids like a cheesy bake.

Sausage & Lentil Casserole

SIMPLICITY:

SERVES:
6 children
or a family of 4

PREP TIME:
30 minutes

COOKING TIME:
1 hour 30 minutes

Most children like sausages – I know mine do. This great recipe encourages even the fussiest eaters to eat lentils as well, which are full of fibre and goodness for growing children.

INGREDIENTS

6 sausages (about 400g/14 oz)

2 tablespoons olive oil

1 onion, peeled and finely chopped

2 garlic cloves, crushed

225g (7 oz) green lentils, rinsed and drained

4 sprigs of fresh thyme, tied with kitchen string

1 bay leaf

2 x 400g (14 oz) tins chopped tomatoes

500ml (18 fl. oz) water

$1/2$ teaspoon freshly ground black pepper

1 teaspoon red wine vinegar

2 tablespoons chopped fresh flat-leaf parsley

- Cook the sausages according to the packet directions. Cool and slice into bite-sized chunks.

- Meanwhile, heat the oil over medium heat in a large, heavy-based saucepan or casserole dish with a lid. Add the onion and garlic and cook for about 6-8 minutes, until the onion is translucent. Be careful not to let the onion or garlic brown.

- Add the sausage, lentils, thyme, bay leaf and chopped tomatoes. Pour in the cold water to cover the contents of the pan and season with the pepper. Bring to the boil then turn the heat down as low as possible and simmer, covered, for about 1 hour, until the lentils are tender. Add more liquid if the lentils start to dry out. Remove the lid and simmer for a further 15-20 minutes.

- Discard the thyme. Stir in the vinegar and parsley before serving.

Try to find organic or free-range sausages with no additives, fillers or nitrates.

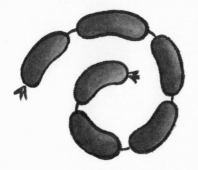

Pork Fillet

A dish that can be thrown together in minutes. Allow a couple of hours for the pork to marinate in the refrigerator to get a wonderfully tender result.

INGREDIENTS

500g (1lb) pork fillet
1 tablespoon hoisin sauce
2 tablespoons soy sauce
1 tablespoon orange juice
1 tablespoon rice wine vinegar
2 garlic cloves, crushed
Olive oil, for coating

- Rinse the pork under cold water, pat dry, then trim away any fat or gristle.

- Combine the hoisin, soy, orange juice, rice wine vinegar and garlic in a large zip-top plastic bag or a bowl; add the pork and seal and marinate in the refrigerator for at least 2 hours.

- Preheat the oven to 200°C/400°F/Gas 6.

- Remove the pork from the bag or bowl, reserving the marinade. Coat the rack of a roasting tin in olive oil. Place the pork on the rack and roast for 18–20 minutes until cooked through: it should be pink in the middle. Cover the pork with foil, place on a cutting board and let it stand for 10 minutes. Cut into slices, roughly 1cm ($^{1}/_{2}$ in) thick.

- Pour the reserved marinade into a small saucepan and bring to the boil. Cook for a couple of minutes to reduce down, and serve with the pork.

Delicious served with Marta's Rice and Peas (page 112) and a green vegetable.

Vegetarian

Omelette

SIMPLICITY:

SERVES:
2–3 children or 1 adult

PREP TIME:
5 minutes

COOKING TIME:
5 minutes

Omelettes are genius. They work for breakfast, lunch or dinner. This is my husband's recipe, which in my opinion rivals the best of any French bistro.

INGREDIENTS

3 eggs
Splash of whole milk
Freshly ground black pepper
25g (1 oz) unsalted butter
50g (2 oz) Cheddar cheese, grated

• Beat the eggs with the milk and a little freshly ground pepper.

• Put a 20cm (8 in) frying or omelette pan over a medium-high heat and add the butter once the pan is hot. Swirl the butter across the pan, then pour in the egg mixture. Cook for about 30 seconds–1 minute, then use a rubber spatula to move the edges towards the centre, so they don't stick to the pan.

• Cook for a further 2–3 minutes so the omelette is almost set but still slightly runny in the middle. Add the cheese and flip one side over to cover it. Cook for 30 seconds, then flip the whole omelette over. Remove from the heat once the cheese has melted.

This omelette is also good with sautéed mushrooms, courgette or spinach which can be added just before the cheese.

Simple Tomato Sauce for Pasta

You'll never feel the need to buy pasta sauce again once you've tried this delicious and quick recipe. It's an essential basic and easy to adapt to other dishes as well as pasta. I tend to freeze it in large batches.

INGREDIENTS
2 tablespoons olive oil
1 medium onion, peeled and chopped
4 garlic cloves, crushed
2 x 400g (14 oz) tins chopped tomatoes
Freshly ground black pepper

- Heat the olive oil in a saucepan over medium-high heat. Add the onion and garlic, stirring occasionally for about 2–3 minutes, until soft. Add the tomatoes and season with black pepper.

- Cook for about 10–15 minutes, stirring occasionally, until mixture thickens.

SIMPLICITY:

SERVES:
6 children or
family of 4

PREP TIME:
5 minutes

COOKING TIME:
10–15 minutes

Leftovers can be frozen for 30 days.

Aubergine Parmigiana

SIMPLICITY:

SERVES:
8 children or a family
of 4 with leftovers

PREP TIME:
25-30 minutes

COOKING TIME:
30-40 minutes

This recipe is lovely on its own or as a side dish.

If your children like pasta, this recipe will probably be a hit. The texture and flavour is similar to lasagne but a welcome vegetarian alternative if you feel they need a break from red meat.

INGREDIENTS
2 tablespoons olive oil
2 garlic cloves, crushed
2 x 400g (14 oz) tins chopped tomatoes
1 teaspoon dried oregano
2 large aubergines (or 3 medium-sized ones)
1 small bunch fresh basil leaves, chopped
Freshly ground black pepper
250g (9 oz) mozzarella cheese, sliced
50g (2 oz) freshly grated Parmesan cheese

- Preheat the oven to 180°C/350°F/Gas 4.

- Make the tomatoe sauce. Heat the olive oil in a saucepan, add the garlic and gently cook for 2 minutes. Add the tomatoes and oregano, bring to the boil, then turn the heat down and simmer for 15 minutes, until the sauce thickens.

- Meanwhile, slice the aubergines into rounds 1cm ($^1/_2$ in) thick. Brush both sides with oil and sauté in a non-stick frying pan, turning a few times until very soft. It's important to get the aubergine as tender as possible, so take extra time if needed.

- Stir the chopped basil into the tomato sauce and season with a couple of grinds of black pepper. Spread a few spoonfuls of sauce across the bottom of an ovenproof dish. Place about a third of the aubergines in a layer over the sauce. Cover with a layer of mozzarella (again, about a third) and sprinkle with Parmesan cheese. Repeat twice more, and end with a thin layer of sauce. Cover with the remaining Parmesan and bake for 30–40 minutes until bubbling.

Macaroni Cheese

Kids and adults both come back for seconds with this dish. I find it's such a treat you can mix in green vegetables with little resistance. Children love to get involved in the simple preparation, if only to snack on the cheese along the way.

INGREDIENTS
250g (9 oz) macaroni
40g (1 ½ oz) unsalted butter
40g (1 ½ oz) plain flour
560ml (1 pint) whole milk
250g (9 oz) Cheddar cheese, grated
50g (2 oz) freshly grated Parmesan cheese

- Cook the macaroni according to the directions on the packet. Drain and set aside.

- Melt the butter in a saucepan over medium heat and whisk in the flour until smooth. Slowly whisk in the milk, stirring the whole time so it doesn't become lumpy. When all the milk has been added, bring to the boil, then turn the heat down and simmer, continuing to stir until thick enough to coat the spoon or whisk. Lower the heat and add two thirds of the Cheddar cheese and stir for a further 3 minutes, until the sauce is thick and smooth.

- Mix the cooked macaroni into the sauce. Put in an oven-proof dish and sprinkle with the remaining Cheddar and the Parmesan cheese. Place under a hot grill and cook for about 5 minutes, until the cheese is browned and bubbling.

Serve on its own, mixed with peas or broccoli, or as a popular side for chicken, meat or fish.

Marta's Rice & Peas

SIMPLICITY:

SERVES:
2–3 children

PREP TIME:
5 minutes

COOKING TIME:
20–25 minutes

Marta has contributed a few recipes to this book. This one is an easy side dish which can be served with chicken, fish or meat. My family likes it with a sprinkling of grated Parmesan cheese on top.

INGREDIENTS

2 tablespoons olive oil

1/4 small onion, peeled and chopped

1 small garlic clove, crushed

125g (4 1/2 oz) basmati rice

125g (4 1/2 oz) peas, fresh or frozen and thawed

300ml (10 fl. oz) vegetable stock (page 29) or shop-
  bought with no added salt, or water

Knob of unsalted butter

- Heat the oil in a saucepan with a lid, add the onion and garlic and cook over a medium heat for 5 minutes, until the onion is slightly golden and soft. Then add the rice and peas and cook for 1 minute. Pour in the vegetable stock (or water), stir well and cover. Cook on a low heat until the rice gradually absorbs all the water.

- Once the rice is cooked through, stir in the butter. For older children and adults season to taste.

Serve with Easy Fish in Foil (page 50) or Pork Fillet (page 102).

Ratatouille Bake

SIMPLICITY:

SERVES:
8 children or a family
of 4 with leftovers

PREP TIME:
10–15 minutes

COOKING TIME:
40 minutes

If your family likes
a bit of spice, add ¼
teaspoon chilli flakes
along with the herbs

I like this ratatouille recipe because it works as a
side dish or can be a hearty vegetarian meal on its
own. This recipe uses quick-cook rice.

INGREDIENTS

2 tablespoons olive oil

2 medium courgettes, sliced into rounds

1 medium aubergine, cubed

1 large onion, peeled and sliced

1 red pepper, sliced into bite-size pieces

1 teaspoon dried oregano

1 teaspoon dried basil or mixed herbs

185g (6.6 oz) quick-cook rice

400g (14 oz) chopped tomatoes (1 tin)

**250ml (9 fl. oz) vegetable stock (page 29) or shop-
bought with no added salt, or water**

90g (3 oz) feta cheese, crumbled

- Preheat the oven to 190°C/375°F/Gas 5.

- Heat the olive oil in a flameproof casserole dish over a medium heat. Add the courgette, aubergine, onion, red pepper and herbs, and sauté for 1–2 minutes.

- Add the rice and sauté for 3 minutes. Then stir in the tomatoes and vegetable stock (or water) and bring to the boil. Add the cheese, cover the dish, transfer to the oven and bake for 40 minutes, until the rice is cooked.

Penne with Green Sauce

SIMPLICITY:

SERVES:
8 children or
a family of 4

PREP TIME:
10 minutes

COOKING TIME:
20-25 minutes

A quick recipe which combines pasta - usually a winner with children - and broccoli, the ultimate super food. This dish works as a simple main but even better as a side to chicken, fish or meat. The garlic and Parmesan combination is tasty enough for younger children, but for older children and adults you'll want to season to taste.

INGREDIENTS

300g (10 oz) wholewheat penne
375g (13 oz) broccoli florets
A few tablespoons of olive oil
3-4 garlic cloves, crushed
Freshly ground black pepper
120ml (4 fl. oz) water
80g (3 oz) freshly grated Parmesan cheese
1 tablespoon finely chopped fresh flat-leaf parsley
  (optional)

- Bring a pan of water to the boil for the pasta. Add the penne and cook according to the directions on the packet. Drain and return to pan.

- Meanwhile, wash the broccoli and chop the florets well (discard stem ends). In a saucepan heat a few tablespoons of olive oil and the garlic over medium heat until the garlic starts to sizzle. Stir in the chopped broccoli and freshly ground black pepper. Add the water and cook, covered, for 20-25 minutes, until the broccoli is very tender and easily mashed – the texture should be very soft. Add more water if needed.

- When the broccoli resembles a 'green sauce' add it to the pasta, then stir in the Parmesan cheese and parsley (if using).

For older children and adults, add a pinch or two of chilli flakes for a bit of spice.

Green Pie

SIMPLICITY:

SERVES:
8 children or a family
of 4 with leftovers

PREP TIME:
20-25 minutes

COOKING TIME:
50-60 minutes

Anything involving pastry piques Monty's interest, which is how I first got him to try this recipe. It's a great way to get kids to eat spinach, a highly nutritious food full of vitamins, zinc and iron. Serve this on its own as a light meal or in a smaller portion as a side dish to chicken, fish or meat.

INGREDIENTS

2 tablespoons olive oil

2 medium onions, peeled and sliced

1 teaspoon freshly ground black pepper

100g (3 ½ oz) unsalted butter, melted

6 sheets filo pastry (about 270g/9 ½ oz),
  defrosted

260g (10 oz) frozen chopped spinach, defrosted

6 large eggs, beaten

Large pinch of freshly grated nutmeg

100g (3 ½ oz) freshly grated Parmesan cheese

40g (1 ½ oz) fresh breadcrumbs (1 slice of brown bread)

225g (8 oz) feta cheese, cut into small cubes

- Preheat the oven to 190°C/375°F/Gas 5.

- Warm the olive oil in a saucepan over a medium heat, then
  sauté the onions for 10–15 minutes, until they are slightly
  browned. Season with the pepper and allow to cool slightly.

- Meanwhile, butter a non-stick, ovenproof pie dish and line
  it with 6 stacked sheets of filo pastry, brushing each one
  with the melted butter and letting the edges hang over the
  sides of the dish.

- Squeeze the spinach to get rid of as much liquid as possible.
  In a bowl combine the spinach with the onions, eggs, nutmeg,
  Parmesan, breadcrumbs and feta. Put the mixture in the
  middle of the pastry and neatly fold the edges over the top
  to seal in the filling.

- Brush the top of the pie with melted butter and bake for 1
  hour, until the top is golden and the filling is set. Allow to
  cool before serving.

**Children can get
involved in the prepa-
ration of this dish:
squeezing out the
spinach, mixing or
helping to fold the
pastry.**

Lentil Soup

SIMPLICITY:

SERVES:
8 children or a family
of 4 with leftovers

PREP TIME:
20 minutes

COOKING TIME:
35-40 minutes

This soup is not difficult to make and seems to impress everyone who tries it, even those you wouldn't expect to enjoy a meat-free meal. The flavour is great and both my children love it.

INGREDIENTS

2 tablespoons olive oil

1 large onion, peeled and chopped

2 medium carrots, peeled and chopped

1 red or yellow pepper, chopped

3 garlic cloves, crushed

1 x 400 g (14 oz) tin chopped tomatoes

1 bay leaf

1 teaspoon fresh thyme leaves

200g (7 oz) Puy lentils, rinsed

Freshly ground black pepper

**1.35 litres (2 pints 8 fl. oz) vegetable stock (page 29) or
shop-bought with no added salt**

360ml (12 fl. oz) water

1 $\frac{1}{2}$ teaspoons balsamic vinegar

- Heat the olive oil in a large pot or casserole dish with a lid and add the onion, carrots and pepper; cook over medium heat for about 2 minutes, stirring occasionally, until the vegetables begin to soften. Add the garlic and cook for about 1 minute, until fragrant. Stir in the tomatoes, bay leaf and thyme and cook for about 1 minute, until fragrant.

- Stir in the lentils and add freshly ground pepper to taste, cover, reduce the heat, and cook for 8–10 minutes, until the vegetables have softened.

- Uncover, increase the heat and add the vegetable stock and water. Bring to the boil, then cover partially and reduce the heat. Simmer for 30–35 minutes, until the lentils are tender but still hold their shape; discard the bay leaf.

- Purée approximately 700ml (1 1/4 pints) of the soup with a hand blender until smooth, then return to the pot. Stir in the balsamic vinegar and cook for a further 5 minutes.

This recipe can be made up to 2 days in advance: simply cool to room temperature and refrigerate. Leftovers can be frozen for 30 days.

Spanish Tortilla

SIMPLICITY:

SERVES:
6 children or family of 4

PREP TIME:
10 minutes

COOKING TIME:
10–15 minutes

This recipe is very popular with children and can be served hot or made in advance. My family likes it best at room temperature. An easy way to flip the tortilla is to put a large plate on top of the frying pan and simply turn over, so the plate is on the bottom and the pan is on top. Lift off the pan and then carefully slide the inverted tortilla back into the pan.

INGREDIENTS
3 tablespoons olive oil
2 medium potatoes, peeled and finely diced
5 large eggs
$^1/_2$ small onion, finely diced
50g (2 oz) Cheddar cheese, grated
2 tablespoons roughly chopped fresh flat-leaf parsley

- Heat 2 tablespoons of the olive oil in a frying pan and sauté the potatoes until they are golden. Transfer the potatoes to a plate lined with kitchen paper to dry them off.

- In a bowl, beat the eggs, then mix in the onion, cheese, parsley and sautéed potatoes.

- Return the frying pan to the heat, add the remaining oil and pour in the mixture. Cook over a medium-low heat for about 5-8 minutes, then flip the tortilla and cook it on the other side for another 5 minutes, until done.

Warm tortilla is great served with sautéed spinach or a steamed green vegetable. If you fancy adding meat, stir in 90g (3 oz) of diced, cooked chorizo to the egg mixture along with the cooked potatoes.

Broccoli, Leek & Cauliflower Bake

SIMPLICITY:

SERVES:
8 children or
a family of 6

PREP TIME:
15-20 minutes

COOKING TIME:
15 minutes

I originally served this to my children because they love anything with cheese. It was a huge hit with them, and my husband and I enjoyed it too. It's a vegetarian dish that is good enough for a main meal but can also be served as a side dish to fish, chicken or meat.

INGREDIENTS

275g (10 oz) cauliflower, cut into small florets

225g (8 oz) broccoli, cut into small florets

2 leeks, thinly sliced

50g (2 oz) butter

50g (2 oz) plain flour

450ml (16 fl. oz) whole milk

175g (6 oz) mild Cheddar cheese, grated

1 tablespoon wholegrain mustard

Pinch of nutmeg

40g (1 ¹/₂ oz) fresh breadcrumbs (1 slice of
  brown bread)

1 tablespoon finely chopped fresh flat-leaf parsley

25g (1 oz) freshly grated Parmesan cheese

- Preheat the oven to 190°C/375°F/Gas 5.

- Add the cauliflower to a saucepan of boiling water and simmer, covered, for 4 minutes. Add the broccoli and leek to the pan, cover and simmer for a further 2–3 minutes. Then drain the vegetables.

- To make the sauce, melt the butter in a saucepan, add the flour and mix together. Gradually pour in the milk while whisking and gently bring to the boil. Cook for 2–3 more minutes, stirring all the time, while the mixture thickens. Mix in the Cheddar cheese, mustard and nutmeg. Remove from the heat and continue to mix until all the cheese has melted.

- Spread the vegetables evenly in an ovenproof dish and pour the cheese sauce on top. Mix the breadcrumbs, parsley and Parmesan cheese together and sprinkle over the top. Bake in the oven for 15 minutes, until golden and slightly crispy.

Treats & Puddings

THERE ONCE WAS A COW CALLED MAY
WHO FANCIED A PUDDING ONE DAY
WITHOUT GETTING FLUSTERED
SHE WHIPPED UP A CUSTARD
AND GOBBLED IT UP, HOORAY!

And now we come to the best part of the book, or what would certainly be my son Monty's favourite section. Here you'll find some of the most fun recipes to make with your children.

In our household, cake is the treat of choice. Nothing brings more delight to my children's faces and it is lovely to see. We have expanded our repertoire to include healthy fruit muffins, cupcakes, apple crumble and chocolate brownies, all of which we've included here, along with some favourites from friends and family.

Choosing the right treats

Treats are an important part of childhood – as long, of course, as they are part of a balanced diet and served in moderation. Monty inherited his father's sweet tooth and loves all puddings (especially his grandmother's homemade cakes). As far as possible, we stick to treats and puddings made from 100 per cent natural ingredients and which don't contain unnecessarily high levels of sugar. Unfortunately there are a great many over-processed biscuits and sweets around in the shops, attracting young children's attention. It's wise to avoid the products (sweet or otherwise) made with additives, preservatives and E numbers, especially for younger children.

It's especially nice to prepare your own treats and puddings: you know exactly what ingredients go into them and it's great fun for the children to be involved. Most children will jump at the opportunity to join in making the following recipes.

French Toast

French Toast is a great breakfast treat on a Saturday or Sunday morning and is quick and simple to make.

INGREDIENTS
1 large egg
2 tablespoons whole milk
¹/₂ teaspoon cinnamon
2 thick slices of brown bread
Knob of butter
Maple syrup, to serve

- In a wide, shallow bowl, beat the egg with the milk and add the cinnamon. Soak the bread on both sides in the egg.

- Melt the butter in a frying pan over medium heat. Add the soaked bread and cook for 2 minutes on each side, until crisp and golden. Serve with maple syrup.

SIMPLICITY:

SERVES:
2 children

PREP TIME:
5 minutes

COOKING TIME:
4 minutes

Fresh Fruit Muffins

SIMPLICITY:

MAKES:
12 muffins

PREP TIME:
10 minutes

COOKING TIME:
20 minutes

This is one of the first recipes I made with Monty, and now that Ridley is almost a year old he sits in his high chair watching us intently as we mix the ingredients together. There is not too much sugar so it's a nice treat to make with younger children.

INGREDIENTS

125g (4 ¹/₂ oz) plain flour

60g (2 ¹/₄ oz) wholemeal flour

60g (2 ¹/₄ oz) rolled oats

60g (2 ¹/₄ oz) brown sugar

3 teaspoons baking powder

60g (2 ¹/₄ oz) blueberries

**60g (2 ¹/₄ oz) peeled and chopped apple
  (about 1 piece of fruit)**

2 medium eggs

180ml (6 fl. oz) milk, plus a little extra if needed

40g (1 ¹/₂ oz) unsalted butter, melted

- Preheat the oven to 190°C/375°F/Gas 5. Grease a 12-hole muffin tin or line with paper cases.

- Mix the dry ingredients together in a large bowl. Add the fresh fruit and toss briefly so it gets a little coating of flour.

- Beat the eggs, milk and melted butter together, then pour over the dry ingredients. Fold lightly together, adding a touch more milk if the mixture feels a little dry. Don't over-beat: the batter should be lumpy and moist, not smooth.

- Spoon the batter into the muffin tin, filling each hole/paper case about two-thirds full, and bake until cooked in the middle, about 20 minutes. Remove from oven and let rest for 10 minutes before taking the muffins out of the tin.

Also very good with raspberries and pears substituted for the blueberries and apple.

Baked Apples

SIMPLICITY:

SERVES:
4 adults or
6-8 children sharing

PREP TIME:
5 minutes

COOKING TIME:
20-30 minutes

This healthy dessert is still special enough to be called a 'treat'. Be sure to cook the apples long enough so they are soft. In fact, this recipe is difficult to overcook, so it's better to allow extra time in the oven rather than too little.

INGREDIENTS
4 small Bramley apples
1 handful raisins
1-2 tablespoons soft brown sugar
4 pinches cinnamon or nutmeg
Knob of unsalted butter

- Preheat the oven to 180°C/350°F/Gas 4.

- Remove the core from each apple and slit the skin around the middle (the equator). Fill the empty cores with raisins, brown sugar, a pinch of cinnamon or nutmeg and a knob of butter each.

- Place on an oven tray and bake for 20-30 minutes, until the apples are tender. Don't undercook: they should look very soft and collapsible when done.

- Leave to cool for 5 minutes before serving as the insides will be very hot!

Serve on their own or with Vanilla Pouring Custard (page 148) or vanilla ice cream.

Pink Ice Cream

Making ice cream may sound like time-consuming labour, but this version is easy to make. It's a huge hit with children, and I have also served it at an adult dinner party with great success.

SIMPLICITY:

SERVES:
8 children or a family of 4 with leftovers

PREP TIME:
15 minutes

COOKING TIME:
no cooking required

INGREDIENTS
450g (1lb) frozen raspberries
2 egg whites
225g (8 oz) granulated sugar
20ml (2 dessertspoons) lemon juice
240ml (8 ½ fl. oz) lightly whipped double cream

- Mix all the ingredients, apart from the cream, in a food processor. The mixture will treble in volume and look quite pink. Make sure you use raspberries straight from the freezer.

- Stir in the whipped cream with a metal spoon and freeze overnight. That's it – ice cream!

Serve the ice cream on its own or topped with fresh fruit.

Grandma's Lemon Cake

SIMPLICITY:

SERVES:
8–10

PREP TIME:
15 minutes

COOKING TIME:
45–50 minutes

When Grandma comes to visit, she always brings one of her delicious homemade cakes. Monty immediately runs to her bag to try to find the cake tin. He loves all Grandma's cake recipes but has a special fondness for this lovely lemon one.

INGREDIENTS
175g (6 oz) unsalted butter at room temperature
175g (6 oz) caster sugar
3 large eggs
Juice and grated rind of 1 lemon
200g (7 oz) self-raising flour
30g (just over 1 oz) ground almonds
1 tablespoon boiled water

For the glaze topping:
6 tablespoons icing sugar, sifted
2 tablespoons lemon juice

- Preheat the oven to 180°C/350°F/Gas 4. Lightly grease a 22 x 11 cm (9 x 4 $^1/_2$ in) loaf tin.

- Cream the butter and sugar together until light and fluffy. This is much quicker if you use an electric beater. If beating by hand, be prepared to beat for at least 5 minutes. Add the eggs one at a time and beat in, then add the lemon juice and rind.

- Fold in the flour and ground almonds. Stir in the tablespoon of boiled water to bring the mixture to a smooth consistency.

- Pour the cake mixture into the loaf tin and bake for 45–50 minutes, until well risen and golden and its aroma fills the kitchen.

- Make the glaze topping. Mix the icing sugar and lemon juice. The consistency will be quite runny. Pour the glaze topping over the cake while it is still in the tin, immediately after it comes out of the oven. Leave it in the tin until cool.

If you are making this for younger children, you can skip the glaze topping and it's still a treat.

Carrot Cake

SIMPLICITY:

SERVES:
8 children

PREP TIME:
15 minutes

COOKING TIME:
45-50 minutes

This recipe is a favourite with Monty's cousins, and in our household too. It is not very sweet, though, and while children seem to love it, some older palates have told me to add more sugar. I have resisted as I think it is great the way it is.

INGREDIENTS

Butter, for greasing
100g (3 ½ oz) light muscovado sugar
150ml (5 fl. oz) sunflower oil
2 large eggs
125g (4 ½ oz) plain wholemeal flour
125g (4 ½ oz) plain flour
2 teaspoons baking powder
1 teaspoon mixed spice
Juice of 1 orange, or 100ml (3 fl. oz) orange juice
2 ripe bananas, mashed
125g (4 ½ oz) carrots, peeled and grated
60g (generous 2 oz) raisins or sultanas

- Preheat the oven to 180°C/350°F/Gas 4. Lightly grease an 18cm (7in) cake tin with butter.

- In a bowl, beat the sugar and oil together with a wooden spoon until smooth, then beat in the eggs, one at a time. Sift in the flour, then add baking powder, mixed spice, orange juice and stir in well. Fold in the banana, carrots and sultanas or raisins.

- Pour the mixture into the cake tin and bake for 45-50 minutes, until the cake is well risen and firm to touch. Let the cake cool for a few minutes, then turn out on to a wire rack to cool.

The icing for the Banana Cupcakes (page 140) works well on this cake. Just make sure to cool the cake completely before icing it.

Banana Cupcakes

SIMPLICITY:

MAKES:
12 cupcakes

PREP TIME:
25 minutes

COOKING TIME:
20-25 minutes

A great way to use up overripe bananas. Children love peeling and mashing the banana, pouring in the ingredients and helping out with the stirring. Use paper cases for easy clean-up.

INGREDIENTS

Butter, for greasing

200g (7 oz) plain wholemeal flour

¹/₄ teaspoon baking soda (bicarbonate of soda)

¹/₄ teaspoon baking powder

90g (3 oz) unsalted butter at room temperature

150g (5 oz) caster sugar

2 large eggs, lightly beaten

3 medium-sized ripe bananas, mashed

For the icing:

200g (7 oz) cream cheese

1 teaspoon vanilla extract

80g (3 oz) icing sugar, sifted

- Preheat the oven to 180°C/350°F/Gas 4. Lightly grease a 12-hole muffin tin or line with paper cases.

- Combine the flour, baking soda and baking powder in a bowl. In a separate large bowl, beat the butter and sugar with a wooden spoon until combined well and there are no lumps. Add the flour mixture and blend well using a whisk. The consistency will be dry and a bit crumbly. Next, stir in the eggs, then fold in the mashed bananas.

- Spoon the mixture into the muffin tin, filling each hole/paper case no more than about two-thirds full. Bake for 20–25 minutes, until well risen and golden brown on top. Cool in tin for 5 minutes, then take out and cool completely on wire rack before icing.

- To make the icing, ensure the cream cheese is cold and put in a bowl. Beat in the vanilla extract until just blended. Gradually beat in the icing sugar until smooth. It's best to use well-sifted icing sugar so you don't get any lumps. Using a knife, spread on the cooled cupcakes.

These cupcakes are sweet enough to serve without the icing, especially for younger children.

Chocolate Brownies

I don't have the same sweet tooth my husband does (and now our children do), but I have a weakness for chocolate brownies. I'm constantly asked for this recipe, and there are never any leftovers.

INGREDIENTS
200g (7 oz) dark chocolate
175g (6 oz) unsalted butter
200g (7 oz) golden caster sugar
150g (5 oz) plain flour
2 handfuls of sultanas, chopped
3 large eggs

- Preheat the oven to 170°C/325°F/Gas 3. Line a 20 x 20 cm (8 x 8 in) baking tray with greaseproof or parchment paper.

- Melt the chocolate and butter in a large heatproof bowl over a saucepan of simmering water until it is smooth. Take the bowl off the heat, add the sugar and, using a wooden spoon, stir until thoroughly mixed in. Stir in the flour and sultanas and finally beat in the eggs.

- The mixture should be thick, glossy and smooth. When ready, pour it into the baking tray and cook for 30-35 minutes. It should have a slightly crunchy top but still be gooey in the middle.

This recipe also works well if you substitute 50g of ground almonds for 50g of the plain flour.

Eton Mess

SIMPLICITY:

SERVES:
8 children or a family
of 4 with leftovers

PREP TIME:
15 minutes

COOKING TIME:
no cooking required

This is a perfect dish for the summer when strawberries are at their best. However, it's such fun to make with children that we use it year-round with whatever fruit we can get. Monty loves to help me crush the meringues.

INGREDIENTS
480ml (17 fl. oz) double cream
1/2 teaspoon vanilla extract
250g (9 oz) strawberries, hulled and sliced
175g (6 oz) raspberries
1 tablespoon Demerara sugar
1 teaspoon balsamic vinegar
125g (4 1/2 oz) meringues

- Whip the cream in a bowl until firm, then stir in the vanilla extract. In a separate bowl combine half the fruit, the sugar and balsamic vinegar, and mash with a fork until the consistency resembles stewed fruit.

- Crush the meringues into pieces.

- In a serving dish, roughly mix together the cream, mashed fruit and crumbled meringues. Scatter the rest of the fruit on top and serve at once.

This can also be made without the Demerara sugar as the meringue contributes a lot of sweetness.

Best eaten the same day, but leftovers are still delicious, if sometimes a bit soggy.

Apple Crumble

SIMPLICITY:

SERVES:
8 children or a family of
4 with leftovers

PREP TIME:
15 minutes

COOKING TIME:
35 minutes

This recipe is especially good in the autumn when apples are in season, however you can make it year-round with seasonal fruit. I've made a more healthy topping than the traditional one, using oats, wholemeal flour and flaxseed. My family loves it and have no idea about the extra fibre and Omega 3 I've snuck in.

INGREDIENTS

For the base:
8 cooking apples, peeled and chopped
Juice of 1/2 lemon
1 tablespoon soft brown sugar
1/2 teaspoon ground cinnamon
1/2 teaspoon nutmeg

For the topping:
100g (3 1/2 oz) rolled porridge oats
100g (3 1/2 oz) plain flour
100g (3 1/2 oz) soft brown sugar
15g (1/2 oz) plain wholemeal flour
2 teaspoons flaxseed
1/2 teaspoon ground cinnamon
120g (4 oz) unsalted butter, cubed

- Preheat the oven to 200°C/400°F/Gas 6.

- For the base: combine the apples, lemon juice, brown sugar, cinnamon, and nutmeg in a bowl and toss together. Put the mixture into a lightly greased deep baking dish, about 20 x 20 cm (8 x 8 in).

- For the topping: combine all the dry ingredients and rub in the butter, using your hands or a fork, until the consistency becomes crumbly. Sprinkle the topping over apples and bake for 35 minutes, until the fruit is bubbling and the topping is browned.

Delicious with Vanilla Pouring Custard (page 148) or vanilla ice cream.

Vanilla Pouring Custard

SIMPLICITY:

MAKES:
1 litre (1 ³/₄ pints)

PREP TIME:
10 minutes

COOKING TIME:
5 minutes

This is my mother's recipe from America and something we always make at Christmas time. I remember my grandparents drinking this during the holidays with a bit of rum. I introduced it to my husband, who was used to thicker, traditional English custards; he poured it over bananas and became an immediate fan. It starts out with a thin consistency, but once you add cornflour it will thicken up nicely. Great on its own – my favourite – or as a topping for desserts such as apple crumble.

INGREDIENTS
1 litre (1 ³/₄ pints) whole milk
6 egg yolks
100g (3 ¹/₂ oz) caster sugar
2 tablespoons cornflour
1 teaspoon vanilla extract

- Prepare a saucepan of simmering water. Bring the milk almost to the boil in another saucepan. Lightly beat the egg yolks and sugar in a heatproof bowl. Stir in the scalded milk gradually. Sit the bowl on top of the pan of hot water and stir the mixture constantly until it thickens enough to coat the spoon.

- Mix the cornflour with a small amount of cold water and stir it into the custard while the bowl is still on the heat. If the custard gets lumpy, place the bowl in cold water and beat until smooth.

- Take the custard off the heat and stir in the vanilla extract.

Simple Greek Yoghurt Puddings

SIMPLICITY:

SERVES:
5 children

PREP TIME:
10 minutes

COOKING TIME:
no cooking required

I love this recipe because you can throw it together in minutes. These are best when freshly made and served at room temperature.

INGREDIENTS
5 strawberries, hulled and chopped
Small punnet of raspberries
Small punnet of blueberries
500g tub (1lb 2 oz) Greek yoghurt
5 teaspoons muscovado sugar

• Take 5 ramekins or small cups and divide the strawberries, raspberries and blueberries equally between them. Add 100g (3 ½ oz) Greek yoghurt on top of each ramekin and sprinkle with muscovado sugar and leave to sit for 10 minutes.

• The sugar will turn brown and gooey, making these healthy puddings delicious – kids love them!

Recipe Planner

MEAL MATCHERS

Recipes that go well together:

Easy Fish in Foil (page 50)
Ratatouille Bake (page 114)
Broccoli, Leek & Cauliflower
 Bake (page 124)
Marta's Rice & Peas (page 112)

Baked Cod (page 52)
Penne with Green Sauce
 (page 116)

**Monty's Favourite Fish Fingers
 (page 54)**
Simple Tomato Sauce (page 107)
Broccoli, Leek & Cauliflower
 Bake (page 124)

Salmon and Pesto (page 55)
Marta's Rice & Peas (page 112)

Fishcakes (page 56)
Broccoli, Leek & Cauliflower
 Bake (page 124)
Ratatouille Bake (page 114)
Macaroni Cheese (page 110)

Caruso's Chicken (page 66)
Marta's Rice & Peas (page 112)
Broccoli, Leek & Cauliflower
 Bake (page 124)
Aubergine Parmigiana
 (page 108)
Green Pie (page 118)

Chicken Milanese (page 70)
Simple Tomato Sauce (page 107)
Aubergine Parmigiana
 (page 108)

**GG's Chicken Supreme
 (page 78)**
Penne with Green Sauce (page
 116)
Green Pie (page 118)
Ratatouille Bake (page 114)

Turkey Meatballs (page 80)
Simple Tomato Sauce (page 107)
Penne with Green Sauce (page
 116)

Meatloaf (page 90)
Macaroni Cheese (page 110)
Ratatouille Bake (page 114)

Pork Fillet (page 102)
Marta's Rice & Peas (page 112)

**Aubergine Parmigiana
 (page 108)**
Caruso's Chicken (page 66)
Chicken Milanese (page 70)

**Penne with Green Sauce
 (page 116)**
GG's Chicken Supreme (page 78)
Turkey Meatballs (page 80)
Baked Cod (page 52)

Macaroni Cheese (page 110)
Meatloaf (page 90)

Fishcakes (page 56)

Marta's Rice & Peas (page 112)
Easy Fish in Foil (page 50)
Pork Fillet (page 102)

Green Pie (page 118)
Caruso's Chicken (page 66)
GG's Chicken Supreme (page 78)

**Broccoli, Leek & Cauliflower
 Bake (page 124)**
Easy Fish in Foil (page 50)
Monty's Favourite Fish Fingers
 (page 54)
Fishcakes (page 56)

Ratatouille Bake (page 114)
Easy Fish in Foil (page 50)
Fishcakes (page 56)
GG's Chicken Supreme (page 78)
Meatloaf (page 90)

Baked Apples (page 132)
Vanilla Pouring Custard
 (page 148)

Apple Crumble (page 146)
Vanilla Pouring Custard
 (page 148)

Chocolate Brownies (page 142)
Pink Ice Cream (page 132)

Index

Acknowledgements

Much thanks and appreciation to Dean Brown, Jane Hunter, Charlotte Whiting, Nancy Evans and Elisa Onia; without their help, support and advice there would not be a Little Dish Favourites Cookbook.

Thanks also to Elizabeth Sheinkman, Nicky Ross, Mari Roberts, Sarah Hammond and everyone at Hodder & Stoughton, as well as the amazing designer Claudio at Pearlfisher.

And special recognition to the following recipe contributors and testers:

Ann Brown, Marta Da Silva, Dale Graves, Esther Jones and Emma Terry, plus Heather Amos, Nicky Anderson, Tom Benton, Nicky Borland, Hattie Deards, Jo Densley, Linda Duffy, Emma Emery, Amy Englehardt, Kirsty Ferguson, Carolina Field, Kelly Foley, Eliza Gore Brown, Sarah Gore Brown, Jane Hargreaves, Alex Hess, Suzanne Johnson, Gussie Maier, Leslie McChesney, Sarah Miles, Patricia Murphy, Solveig Nepstad, Lesley Onyett, Sue Roberts, Amy Robson, Simone Riches, Monique Seager, Lottie Shaw, Frankie Sheekey, Sarah Smith, Sophie Tomlinson, Nicola Toms, Suzie Uttley, Dave Voss, Charlotte Waters and Claire White.